T0169308

The final end and ultimate return of the gnostics …
is that the Real is identical with them,
while they do not exist.

Ibn 'Arabī[1]

For Love
of the Real

A Story of Life's Mystical Secret

LLEWELLYN VAUGHAN-LEE

with HILARY HART

THE GOLDEN SUFI CENTER

First published in the United States in 2015 by
The Golden Sufi Center
P.O. Box 456
Point Reyes, California 94956
www.goldensufi.org

First paperback edition, 2018

Copyright © 2015, 2018 The Golden Sufi Center.
All rights reserved.
No part of this book may be reproduced or utilized
in any form or by any means, electronic or mechanical,
without permission in writing from the Publisher.

Front cover photo ©John Lawson, Belhaven, Scotland.
Back cover photo ©Astra Takes Photos, "Life in the
Excelsior: The Hut Window."

Printed and bound by Thomson-Shore.

Paperback ISBN 13: 978-1-941394-25-0
Hardcover ISBN 13: 978-1-941394-11-3

Library of Congress Cataloging-in-Publication Data
Vaughan-Lee, Llewellyn.
  For love of the real : a story of life's mystical secret / by Llewellyn
Vaughan-Lee.
     pages cm
  ISBN 978-1-941394-11-3 (hardcover : alk. paper)
1. Mysticism. 2. Sufism. 3. Buddhism. I. Title.
  BL625.V38 2015
  297.4'4--dc23
                        2015017580

This book is printed on 100% post-consumer recycled paper,
FSC Certified, and processed without chlorine.

CONTENTS

Foreword   i

Introduction: *Before the Beginning*   iii

1. Serving the Absolute   1

2. The Hidden Face of God   13

3. The Gift of Nothingness   29

4. Oneness   47

5. Two Poles of Love   65

6. The Magic of Creation   81

7. Veils of Light, Veils of Darkness   97

8. Return to the Real   113

Epilogue: *A Story of Life's Mystical Secret*   127

Notes   131

Index   139

Bibliography   142

Acknowledgments   144

PREFACE

Throughout this book, God, the Great Beloved, is sometimes referred to as He. Of course Absolute Truth is neither
masculine nor feminine. As much as It has a divine masculine
side, so It also has an awe-inspiring feminine aspect. Also the
terms Real, God, and the Absolute are used interchangeably.
They are words for an Ultimate Reality that by Its very nature
is beyond all names.

FOREWORD

—◦◦◦◦◦—

These chapters are based on a series of talks I gave, primarily at the Omega Institute in Rhinebeck, New York, between 2002 and 2008. They explore the central esoteric theme of our relationship to the Real, or Absolute Truth. Expressed here within the context of Sufism and also including Buddhist principles, these teachings are not limited to any one spiritual tradition; rather they belong to the foundation of mysticism. They are part of our deepest human heritage, the stamp of the Divine within the soul.

There is a starkness to these writings that comes from both the nature of the talks and the subject. They are a series of meditations to be gradually absorbed—a wine to be sipped.

I am very grateful to Hilary Hart for her work in editing these talks, helping me to make these teachings accessible. I sincerely hope that they help the reader to return to this essential core that is deep within each of us, to remember what is Real.

Llewellyn Vaughan-Lee,
Inverness, California, 2015

INTRODUCTION

Before the Beginning

————

Before the beginning, where there is neither form nor emptiness, neither existence nor non-existence, is the Real. Inaccessible, unknowable, the Real craved to know Itself, to love Itself, to reveal Itself, and so began the endless and instantaneous journey into what we call existence, what we know as life. On this journey the Real passed through many levels, or planes of manifestation, and through this journey It began to both hide and reveal Itself; for paradoxically, as It became more visible so It became more hidden, as expressed by the great master, Ibn 'Arabī:

> How can I know You when You are
>   the Inwardly Hidden who is not known?
> How can I not know You when You are
>   the outwardly Manifest, making Yourself
>   known to me in everything?[1]

The mystic is one who is drawn to seek the Real—to uncover the Absolute within the play of manifestation, within the wonder and beauty of life, and also to make the return journey through the planes of manifestation, into the primal emptiness and beyond, back to the Source. As a lodestone draws iron, the heart of the mystic is drawn on this impossible quest, all for the sake of the Real. The Absolute draws us back to Itself. And it also opens our eyes to the Real within creation, allows us to see what is hidden within life—life's great secret.

In our world today so much real knowledge has been lost that we are left with just a few traces, fragments remembered only in myths or stories told to children. Like the ancient libraries that have all been burned or destroyed, we have lost the knowing of the names of creation and power of naming. We no longer know the magic that binds the worlds together, just as most women have forgotten their ancient instinctual knowing of the mysteries of creation.

Even our images of spirituality hold just a trace of what is real. Today when people speak of spiritual awakening, they rarely refer to the complete awakening on the plane of the Self, the state of *samadhi* in which there is pure bliss and full consciousness of the limitless love and light that belong to our divine nature. And awakening to the empty void of Non-existence, or the reality of the Absolute, is even further from our collective spiritual consciousness.

And perhaps more importantly, we have forgotten the deepest purpose of being human—how we participate in the unfolding of the Real within and around us.

When so much has been lost and forgotten, the danger is that we will remain caught in patterns of illusion without the ancient tools that can help us understand the real nature and purpose of life. In this darkness of forgetting, in the dying of the light, it is essential to return to what is real and true, to the deepest lodestone of our existence. And in the core of our being we carry the imprint of the Absolute, the one Reality, the Source of all, because without It there would be no existence.

Even when all else has been distorted, this remains— a thread to lead us out of the maze of our forgetfulness. The following pages tell a story of this imprint, this remembrance that is so essential.

It is a journey to the core of our existence, a search for what is Real.

Some may say that there is no need for such a journey or search, that everything around us is real and it is only our patterns of perception that distort. Others may say that everything is an illusion, the endless *samsara* of our existence, that only the Absolute is real. And, paradoxically, both these teachings are true. But there is an older teaching that tells of what was before the beginning, before the patterns of our existence came into being, before even the first breath.

It is a light older than the darkness, a memory from before the mind. There is a need to return to this knowing, and to stay true to its imprint—to its call and our response. And to bring this imprint from the innermost depths back through the veils of creation, back through both the in- and out-breath, back into consciousness, into life.

1

SERVING THE ABSOLUTE

The Absolute is real. It is the only thing that is real.

The Absolute exists throughout every plane of creation and beyond creation in the dynamic dimensions of nothingness. And beyond even nothingness, It is the Source of all that is and is not.

Every cell of creation contains a seed, or a substance, of the Absolute. Existence—what we call the visible world—is the light of the Absolute interacting with this substance. The light of the Absolute, traveling through the planes of nothingness and existence, is reflected off this substance in creation, and returns to the Source.

This world of plants and animals, clouds and soil, beauty and horror, is both a veil and a reflection of the Real. Seen from the level of the ego, it is a veil, an illusion. Experienced through a heart aligned with Truth, it is a place of divine revelation.

Just as the Absolute is a seed in every cell of creation, It is a seed within the hearts of humanity. The heart has a number of different chambers and the central chamber belongs only to the Absolute. In Sufism, this is called the "heart of hearts." This chamber in the heart is a doorway to what is Real. Through the heart of hearts, human beings have the birthright of aligning with the Absolute, of consciously connecting with Truth. This is the hallmark of a human being.

But the Absolute is very purposefully veiled from most of humanity. As T.S. Eliot wrote, "Human kind cannot bear very much reality."[1] Those who have glimpsed Reality without being prepared for it can find themselves over-whelmed. When the veils lift and we see, even for an instant, the brilliance and infinite nature of the Divine, we are thrown out of our ego-self. A fragile ego-consciousness or psyche can easily be shattered by the experience, by a Truth that the mind cannot begin to grasp or understand.

Throughout the ages, spiritual masters have prepared seekers to experience the energy, the power, and the infinite nature of the Absolute through spiritual practices and initiations. These create a container in the consciousness of the seeker to enable her to perceive a higher level of reality without being overwhelmed or damaged by it.[2] Different levels of initiation, a lifetime on the path, guide us nearer and nearer to the Real.

But the rules have changed. Because we are entering a new cycle of evolution and because the needs of humanity are so great, certain gates of grace are open that used to be closed. One of these gates has to do with the mystical connection between the human being and the Absolute, and the need of the Absolute to be used by humanity for the sake of the whole.

Most of humanity cannot have direct access to the Absolute because most people cannot go beyond the ego. The ego and its desires experienced through the world of the senses are all that exist for them. But for those who are drawn to know life *as it is*, those who are drawn to serve the Real, new doorways are opening. These individuals are being called to participate in the tremendous changes taking place in the world—to serve the need of the time and to restore what is Real within life.

But to do so we must remember many things. First and foremost, we must remember that creation has always belonged to the Creator. *The world belongs to God.*

COLLECTIVE FORGETTING

There have been many cultures in which every act was an act of remembrance. The making of bread, the hunting of animals, the telling of stories, the rituals of birth and of death—everything was an interweaving of remembrance in which the worlds came together. Every act was an invitation to or celebration of the Divine, every act an opportunity to nourish the soul.

But our world has become a strange place. It has become a wasteland separated from heaven, an objectified world where only *stuff* matters. It has become a place almost solely of our desires, governed by rational thought and driven by economics. Our world no longer directly reflects the Truth; it reflects us. It reflects the distortions of our ego. It reflects the power drive and greed of humanity rather than that spark within the heart.

The wellsprings of life have been drying up because they are no longer connected to the Absolute. This is not a metaphor. The wellsprings of life are the channels for the Absolute to flow into the world, nourishing life and humanity. Clogged, polluted, distorted, they can no longer flow.

This phenomenon is not new; the 13th-century Sufi poet Fakhruddīn 'Irāqī observed it even in his own time.

3

Referring to Khidr, a figure of divine revelation, he wrote: "That magic spring where Khidr once drank the water of life is in your own home but you have blocked its flow." But now this blocking of the flow of the Absolute to Its world has increased to such a degree that it is killing life. It is not solely ecological issues that are doing the damage. The ecological problems are a reflection of an underlying spiritual problem.

On the highest plane of manifestation—the plane of the Self—and beyond, on the planes of nothingness, there is no pollution. But accessing these planes generally takes many, many years of spiritual training. And experiences on these planes can be easily overwhelming in their intensity. For these reasons, humanity has traditionally worked through the archetypal world of images and symbols. In Sufism this inner world of the imaginal is seen as a bridge, an "intermediary between the world of Mystery (*'ālam al-ghayb*) and the world of visibility (*'ālam al-shahādat*)."[3]

Through this intermediate realm, working with its symbols, individuals can make the spiritual ascent from the physical world to the interior world of the Self. Through it we can have access to and be nourished by the numinous energy of the Divine, without being overwhelmed by its intensity; we are given the *manna* that is a gift from God. This energy gives life its true meaning and primal vitality.

But just as we have polluted the outer world with our endless desires, so have we polluted the inner world, blocking and restricting its flow. We live in a civilization whose materialistic values and total reliance on rationality have denied even the existence of the inner reality that underlies all of creation, whose energies form the "river beds of life."

We have no understanding of how this denial, together with our greed and desires, has made a wasteland of the inner dimensions. Monsters of greed and materialism ravage both the outer and inner worlds. Our forgetfulness of the sacred and our misuse of symbols and images have distorted life on the inner planes as well as the outer.[4] So many places of refuge have been lost, temples of the imaginal destroyed, groves that held sacred earth-energies felled by the clear-cutting of our rational mind.

The anger of the archetypal Feminine, which has suffered centuries of abuse through the patriarchal power structures that have dominated nature without any wisdom or restraint, has also restricted the flow from the inner world. And closer to the planes of manifestation are all the corrupted thought-forms of spiritual seekers trying to use spiritual energy to get something for themselves, to serve their ego-self rather than the Divine.

The old ways of bringing the energy down through the planes gradually, by working with the archetypes and their symbols through active imagination and sacred symbolic ritual, don't work in the same way anymore because these archetypal planes have been distorted. Life energy in the past sparkled with purity, as St. John the Divine observed in his Revelation:

> And he showed me a pure river of the water of
> life, clear as crystal, proceeding from the throne
> of God and of the Lamb.[5]

Now by the time it gets to us, the water of life is no longer pure or healthy; it is polluted, like our drinking water.

In order to restore what has been corrupted, new doorways have had to open. Other pathways into the core of life that bypass those places of corruption have had to be created. Now, humanity has to remember how to work at those places where the inner and outer meet, where the energy of the Absolute comes into creation, so we can participate in how the Absolute restores Its world.

Humanity is being given energy, power, and knowing that can help with this work. The Absolute has direct access anywhere in this world through the heart and soul of a human being. As a human being lives, grounded in this world, aware of its sacred nature, a simple and powerful alignment takes place that can allow the energy of the Absolute to come right into life and go where it is needed. Then it can be used to nourish our dying world.

Nothing else can do it. Because the world has gone beyond the point of return, it has gone beyond the crisis point. Trying to "save the world" might help address some of the problems we face, but any solution would remain only on the level of the problem. There would be no real change, no real transformation.

We know how it works on an individual level. One works on a problem, and perhaps the problem seems resolved. But the underlying disorder remains, and the energy put into the solution often just constellates a problem in another form. Thus, the illusion is repeated. But if you are transformed by grace, by the energy from another plane, then you can leave the problem behind.

The world's problems cannot be solved on the level of the world's problems. There is no technological solution to sustain both our current way of life and the life of the planet. Our civilization and the world itself have to be redeemed on a far deeper level. We need to make a real shift, and for this, energy from beyond the physical and even the archetypal planes is necessary.

With the energy of the Absolute, the world can be re-created from its core, from the very center of its being. The world we have distorted with our desires and greed can return to its essential nature.

LIFE AS THE REAL

To participate in this work, we need to remember a hidden dimension to the mystical path, an aspect that has been forgotten over the last centuries.

There have always been two purposes of the path. The purpose most commonly understood is the path of individual evolution. An individual is attracted to a path because she experiences a calling to go back to the Real, to know her true nature, to live a life beyond the illusions of the ego. The Real has put that calling in the heart of human beings to make this return journey of the soul back to its true Home.

Each mystical path carries a different quality of energy, a different ray of light. Some paths work more through love, others more through beauty or devotion, and others through knowledge, or service. The seeker is attracted to the light that is most accessible or familiar. But in essence they are all a way to return from the world of the ego to our real Source, our divine nature.

But this journey Home is just half of the cycle. There is also the energy of the Absolute flowing back into creation, continually sustaining creation.

7

It is like the breath. On the one hand, there is the in-breath, the journey inward back to the Source. But there is also the out-breath, which is the breath that comes down from the Absolute and out into life.

Every breath contains this cycle. The energy of creation flows down through the planes of manifestation, through the soul, through the body, and then back through the inner to the Absolute. Every breath is the breath of the Absolute. With each cycle, divine love and divine will come into life and then return.

Throughout history, a few mystical traditions have taught not just about the return journey, but also about how to acknowledge and work with the Absolute as it manifests through creation. These traditions have emphasized being present in this world, not rejecting life. By being present on this most primal level of existence, we become the doorway for the Absolute to also be present.

Sufism sees the world as a revelation of the Divine— the Self-disclosure of God. Its teachings offer the means to know the Real in a world that appears to be an illusion. Ibn 'Arabī put this simply when he said, "Engendered being is only imagination, yet in truth it is the Real. He who has understood this point has grasped the mysteries of the Path."[6]

On the one hand, *engendered being* is only imagination. What we think of as life, the way it appears, is only something we create in our minds. But on the other hand, it is the Real. The truth of how this world can be known as Real is one of those things that is very simple and incredibly esoteric at the same time. It is like the sound of one hand clapping. The sound of one hand clapping is so much simpler than the sound of two hands clapping, because the sound of one hand clapping doesn't need motion or noise. *It just is.*

There is a way for a human being to *be* where the worlds come together, where the manifest world is not a dream, not a "dewdrop within a dewdrop," but an expression of the Real.

In the Sufi tradition this is "where the two seas meet," and it is here that we encounter Khidr.[7] Living at this place where the worlds intersect is the acknowledgment of the Real on all planes. This way of living and serving requires great attention and awareness. As the 8th-century Buddhist master Padmasambhava described it,

Though my View is as spacious as the sky,
My actions and respect for cause and effect
    are as fine as grains of flour.

In many traditions, training in how to consciously work with the energy of the Real as it comes into creation was given after twenty or so years of focus on the return journey—the in-breath of the path. This training was only given when the mind, physical body, and emotions were all controlled. But today, there is not time for twenty years of meditation and practice. The need is too great.

Some of us are here to respond to this need. We are not here to focus on solving our own problems; we are not even here to solve our own spiritual problems. We are here to serve.

SERVANTHOOD

The moment we think spiritual life is about us, we identify with the ego, and the ego is an illusion. You cannot know or serve the Absolute through an illusion. The greatest illusion humanity has is our sense of self, ego, separate identity. We are not separate. Reality cannot be separate. The Absolute cannot be separate. There is only One.

This is a simple, fundamental, and easily overlooked principle. The moment you do something solely for yourself you are separate. You identify with yourself. This is why so much of what people call spiritual life or spiritual aspiration veils the individual from the Absolute—because it's about them.

Sufism stresses that the path only begins when we turn away from our self: "Take one step away from yourself and behold, the path."[8] Sufism also stresses that we are here to be of service, we are servants of God. Ibn 'Arabī suggests that servanthood is the only real human existence in relation to the Absolute: "The servant is always the servant. The Lord is always the Lord."[9]

In Sufism, servanthood is understood as an expression of our innate relationship with the Divine, a relationship that is also based upon unity. In a state of servanthood, it is the Beloved within us in service to Its own revelation. It is an unfolding of oneness. It is an opening of oneness.

This nuanced understanding of servanthood is mirrored in the Mahayana tradition of Buddhism, which stresses the role of the Bodhisattva—the individual who foregoes enlightenment to guide others to freedom. The Bodhisattva experience is based on *bodhichitta*, an awakened heart confident in the oneness of form and emptiness.

And it is also mirrored in the wisdom of Mother Teresa, who saw all those she served as Jesus "in disguise." When asked, "How can you take care of so many?" she replied, "I only take care of the One."

The simple act of giving oneself, this simple statement of "I am here for Your sake," opens the doors of grace and attunes the servant to the oneness of life, the union of higher and lower, heaven and earth, sacred and profane. It is in that giving of oneself that one can access the energy of the Absolute. And this energy is available now in ways it has never been. What matters is our attitude: *I am not here for myself. I am not here to get anything. I am here to be in service.*

If we are inwardly aligned and the gates of grace are open and permission has been given, then the power of the Absolute—a power that is love, that binds the worlds together—can come directly through the human being, reconnecting life to its source. Then the Absolute can use us to breathe Itself into life; It can interact directly with this world without going through all the planes of manifestation in which the energy so easily gets blocked or diluted.

There is nothing more beautiful and powerful on this plane than a human being aligned with the Absolute, in service to the Absolute, who wants nothing for herself. A human being aligned with Truth is the most extraordinary energy transmitter. She becomes like an open doorway from the Absolute down to creation. Such a human being becomes the link of love between the worlds.

Once we step into an attitude of servanthood, we are available on whatever plane or dimension we are needed. The Absolute can use us in the emptiness of the void, or to work with love or peace on the planes of the Self, or with the earth-energies manifesting through the natural world. We can work in the visible or invisible worlds, or both.

It is critical to understand that not wanting anything for yourself is not an attitude of rejection or denial. Service is not a denial of yourself; it is an affirmation of Self. It is not a denial of life; it is an affirmation of what is *real* in life. It is not a turning away from existence, but an affirmation of existence alive with oneness and love, spinning in the dazzling darkness of nothingness. It is an affirmation of the Real throughout all the levels of creation.

2

THE HIDDEN FACE OF GOD

*Desert and void. The Uncreated is waste and emptiness
to the creature. Not even sand. Not even stone. Not even
darkness and night. A burning wilderness would at least be
"something." It burns and is wild. But the Uncreated is
no something. Waste. Emptiness. Total poverty of the
Creator; yet from this poverty springs everything.*

Thomas Merton[1]

Almost everything that has been written about spiritual life in the West is about what happens from the plane of pure being down into the planes of manifestation. Awakening to the peace and wholeness of the Self, mindfulness, selfless service, or working with the archetypes and the sacred energies of the Earth—all take place in the realms of existence.

But there is another esoteric science, a very different set of spiritual teachings that have to do with the hidden face of God, the invisible substance of the Absolute that is both here and not here.

Because just as the Absolute is, the Absolute is not.

Human beings have the ability to participate in this hidden, undefinable, invisible emptiness. One can't explain how to do it because it's not a "how to." How can you "do" something with nothing? How can you even find what does not exist?

But it is important to know that the nothingness is real. If we are present in life aligned with the Real, then we are used as we are needed. And some mystics have the capacity to work on the plane of emptiness. There, it is vibrant and very alive, dynamic and free. This is the home of the mystic who is absorbed in a God beyond any image, an Unnamable Essence—those who know "there is nothing but nothingness."

Nothingness is a very powerful dimension because the energy of the Absolute has not been dispersed yet; it hasn't been scattered into fragments, refracted into form.

Consider how sunlight functions. Sunlight streams through the darkness of space where it is invisible. As soon as it hits the plane of manifestation the light refracts into the brilliance of form and color. It is only after light is reflected that it becomes visible, but at that same moment of reflection some quality of the light is lost. If one looks at the leaves of a tree, one is seeing the sunlight reflected from a beautiful form, but the sunlight itself has become diminished. It is no longer as pure—a quality of its essential nature is no longer present.

It is the same with the energy of the Absolute, which is reflected, dispersed, and caught when it hits the plane of manifestation.[2] But in the dimension of nothingness, it remains unconstricted.

There is a way to work with this energy before it is reflected. There is a way to be in nothingness, present and absent, a bridge between dimensions.

Working with nothingness is possible when, for a moment, one steps outside of oneself into the borderland between the here and the there. Surrendering to the

14

emptiness of the inner, to one's essential non-existence, the mystic is no longer constricted by form. Life in its fundamental nature stops being defined and can never be fully defined again. This borderland is filled with primal power, forces of chaos, and currents of energy.

This dynamic space is home to the uncreated, the not-yet-created, and that which was created but is now dissolving.

For centuries, mystics have worked between the worlds, at the intersection of nothing and something, in service to the evolution of the whole. Once energy comes into the plane of manifestation it is not only dispersed but it is harder to work with. It is much denser. It moves more slowly. It has already become defined. Even a thought-form already belongs to the plane of manifestation. While it is easier to change a thought than a building, it is still more difficult than working with energy before it has become constricted by any form at all.

And the void is full of energy. It is a much more powerful energy source than the plane of manifestation. Many, many things are possible in the void that are not possible in the world of forms—it is full of infinite potential. Working with the primal energy of creation *before* it comes into the planes of existence is like a dance of light: unreflected, dark light. And of course, there is tremendous freedom because there are no restrictions—in the emptiness, who or what is there to create any restriction? This work opens the doorway to a whole new realm of possibilities, because if we aren't there then neither are our histories, our prejudices, or our prescriptions for the future.

Working in nothingness gives us access to a dimension free from definitions and free from any form of corruption. And all our definitions belong to the past. If there is any hope for the future—if the future is going to be real—it must be free of the contamination that restricts what is and what will be with what has gone before.

LEVELS OF REALITY

Generally, most people understand nothingness as the opposite of something. We think of "nothingness" as what isn't there. But it appears so only from the view of the ego or the mind; seen from the ego, nothingness is absence or negation. But seen from the void, it is the ego that's empty and lifeless, like a shell.

Nothingness is a powerful dimension quite distinct from all other levels of reality. Every level of reality has its own laws. For example, the law of cause and effect governs the physical plane. As Newton said, every action has an equal and opposite reaction. We see examples of this law all around us.

On the level of the Self, there are different sets of laws. The Self is a plane of oneness, and oneness works differently from the physical world, which is a plane of multiplicity. In oneness, individuals are known by their unique true nature and yet are also one with all life. Working on the plane of the Self, the seeker is one with the teacher and also unique. The Sufi teacher Irina Tweedie used to say to her students: "There, I am you and you are me, and you are you and I am me."

While on the plane of the Self everything is revealed according to its true nature, on the plane of nothingness everything is absorbed back into its very essence. Just as darkness absorbs light, nothingness absorbs and yet at the same time reveals the very essence of what is. Thomas Merton describes this as "the incomparable point":

> But for each of us there is a point of nowhereness in the middle of movement, a point of nothingness in the midst of being; the incomparable point, not to be discovered by insight. If you seek it you do not find it. If you stop seeking, it is there. But you must not turn to it. Once you become aware of yourself as seeker, you are lost. But if you are content to be lost you will be found without knowing it, precisely because you are lost, for you are, at last, nowhere.[3]

In this nowhere, this nothingness, is a greater freedom than can be found on the plane of the Self, for by its very nature existence restricts; it veils and hides.

The plane of nothingness is not separate, it is not "other," but is an integral part of the whole. It might be distinct from the plane of the Self or Soul, but it is not separate from it.

Other cultures have understood the multi-dimensionality of life and allowed different levels of life to work together. In medieval times, for example, humanity knew itself to be within the "great chain of being," in which the physical world was connected to the angelic world, and then the ultimate reality of God. That was the consciousness in which people lived. They lived within a symbolic, multi-dimensional universe.[4]

As part of an interrelated whole, life is free and dynamic, flowing from level to level. Today, we have lost this freedom. We live in a culture limited and defined by the physical world of manifestation, with little or no reference to the inner worlds. Nor do we have much understanding of the effect of this censorship of the inner, how complete and how insidious this conditioning toward "something" is. Culturally we have long dismissed the symbolic world, and our present culture has little time for non-action, little space for emptiness; in its constant clamor silence is rarely heard.

We used to allow the different levels of reality to interact more freely, which allowed for magic and miraculous things to happen. The experience of miracles is the phenomenon of a higher level of reality interceding or influencing another plane. Such experiences are not conditioned by effort; rather they are expressions of grace. Today, we continually solidify the energy of life, demanding that life express itself through things we can see and feel and own. This fundamental materialism has taken a great toll on us as well as on every level of creation, denying both the reality of other dimensions and restricting how all dimensions can work together. We have constricted the flow of life in ways we do not even understand.

In the West, our main spiritual teachings about dimensions beyond the physical plane focus on the dimension of pure being—the Higher Self. This concept of the Self, or soul, is at the root of our Western spiritual consciousness, which is imaged in the figure of Christ. Christ is human and divine, and Christ as an archetype gave to the West a consciousness of our own individual divinity, the part of us that is united with God—"I and my father are one."[5]

Many people have had experiences of the Self, though they may not realize it—"moments in and out of time," as

T.S. Eliot describes them, like "music heard so deeply that it is not heard at all."[6] Moments of stillness, of silence, or of pure presence are also experiences of the Self.

The Self is a state of being. Sometimes this state of being is experienced in meditation. This is the first experience of our higher consciousness—the beginning of *samadhi*. In *samadhi*, there is no movement of consciousness; there is no linear awareness, no before, no after. There just *is*. And it is very, very beautiful, a state of bliss; it is also very dynamic.

Many seekers think of such states as the ultimate spiritual goal. We hope to realize the Higher Self, to become aware of our own divinity—our true nature. And Self-realization *is* a stage along the path. But it is not the end of the journey. It is said that for *Brahmavidya*, the ultimate knowledge of Brahma or absolute universal reality, *Thousands of years and thousands of years are not enough* ... The journey goes on and on; there is no moment of realization after which everything is over. Every stage is just a beginning.

And beyond the Self is what is not.

This dimension of nothingness is always present, and has been present since the beginning of the spiritual search, hidden, but calling the seeker onward.

Everything comes from this desert Nothing.
Everything wants to return to it and cannot.
For who can return "nowhere?"[7]

The moment a seeker is attracted to spiritual life, attracted to a real way of giving oneself, she begins to sense what is not here. The lure of the invisible and unknowable, of a Truth beyond form, draws us inward and to spiritual practices, like meditation, which help train the mind to function in emptiness, in the inner silence. The very fact that one attempts to still the mind means one's consciousness is already aspiring to be present in emptiness, to function at this intersecting plane between something and nothing.

There have been traditions—particularly Buddhist traditions—that have tried to awaken seekers to the dimension of nothingness. In the Heart Sutra, one of the greatest sutras in Mahayana Buddhism, Avalokiteshvara, a Bodhisattva of compassion, explains the paradox of ultimate reality: "Form is emptiness, and emptiness is form; form is no other than emptiness and emptiness is no other than form."

Tokuson, the 9th-century Zen master, offered these instructions: "However deep your knowledge of the scriptures, it is no more than a strand of hair in the vastness of space. However important appears your worldly experience, it is but a drop of water in a deep ravine."

The Sufi path has also historically pointed towards emptiness. Sufism is defined as "Truth without form," and in the words of the Sufi martyr al-Hallāj, "When Truth has taken hold of a heart, she empties it of all but Herself."[8] This is the process of annihilation, *fanā*, that leads to *baqā*, abiding in God.[9] You can only abide in God after you have been annihilated, after you are no longer there. The great Sufi al-Junayd wrote:

> Being wholly present in God, he is wholly lost to self. And thus he is present before God, absent in himself; absent and present at the same time. He is where he is not and he is not where he is.[10]

Abiding in God, absorbed in the Real, the mystic knows that the Higher Self is not an expression of one's own individuality. Rather, the Self is the first differentiation of the primal emptiness, of pure being without form. The Self is like a fulcrum, a point in space between differentiated reality and undifferentiated reality. It is the portal to our own non-existence. And for the Sufi, the heart, home of the Self, is this doorway between the worlds. Through the heart the wayfarer has access to her divine nature and then beyond, to the divine Essence.

But it is a mistake to think that one has to realize the Self, to become stable in an experience of the soul, in order to access nothingness. That would suggest a linear hierarchical framework, and it doesn't work like that. Human beings contain within themselves all levels of existence. We have everything within us, embryonically. Thus, we have access to all the planes of existence and non-existence.

But we must let go of past ideas that the void is separate from us. Just as we have come to understand through the revelations of particle physics that matter exists within a field of invisible dark energy, we can realize that we exist within nothingness. Our existence does not have to be threatened by nothingness. Existence and non-existence work together. Once we consciously have a slightly more correct model, we are able to work with the energies of our own spiritual nature and the spiritual nature of life more in accordance with the way we actually are.

One can sense the nothingness if one is attentive in the right way, in the way one can hear silence. And one can work with emptiness. One works with it through the heart, through the Self.

Everything is present at each moment of time. Life is filled with emptiness. And the emptiness is pulsating with love.

LOVE AND POWER

Within the void is love in its completeness—love that is undifferentiated, unlimited, and very, very pure. Love is the substance of the universe, the substance of life. Love is the greatest power in creation. The energy of love spins the atoms, spins the world, spins the galaxies.

From the perspective of the ego, love can be terrifying. The ego likes attachment, emotion, some passion, and usually some form of codependence—not the limitless freedom, all-demanding intensity, and total commitment of real love. Sadly, most people are only happy with the crumbs from the table of love, not its completeness. Life presents a whole banquet of abundance, yet people crawl around on the floor settling for a few crumbs fallen from the table.

Love is not interested in neuroses or problems. It is too free; it is too potent. Real love subverts your thinking process. It gets between the cracks of your defenses. It is like a perfume; it isn't there and it is there and you want it but you are terrified of it. You long for it even knowing it may cause you unbelievable suffering—you don't care. For the lover it is this invisible fragrance that draws us always deeper into the heart.

Love can lead you not just toward union, but also into nothingness. "Love is a madman," says Rūmī, "working his wild schemes, tearing off his clothes, running through the mountains, drinking poison, and now quietly choosing annihilation."[11]

We need to remember how a heart can be both full and empty at the same time. The very presence of love is also absence. If there is love there is no "you" because you would take up the space where the love is. And yet, the

22

love needs you. You are needed to bring love into the world. Love flows through your heart, and the emptier your heart, the more the love. This love is not you, and yet you are not other than the love.

In the void, love can start to sing, and it sings its own song rather than the song you want it to sing. If you can let love do what it wants to do, then it can take you somewhere else entirely, into the beyond of the beyond, into life's deepest mystical mystery. Here, at the source of the Source is love's deepest truth, which is also our truth.

It is the same with power. In the void, power has not yet been diminished by the structures of creation or the dynamics of human beings. There are no hierarchies or patterns of power, no abuse or misuse. Pure power has the potential to create, transform, and destroy anything and everything—in an instant. It is a primal force.

And in the void, power is love.

One can only access this power if one lets go of old images of power that are no longer helpful. Old models of spiritual power have placed the void somewhere far away, up there, out of reach for most ordinary seekers. There are people who know and people who don't know. There are those with access and those without access.

This hierarchical model does not just separate human beings from the void; it also separates the void from human beings. And separates love from power and power from creation.

But there is no separation and there is no ladder of ascent. There is no spiritual progress. When he was asked about spiritual progress, the Sufi saint Radha Mohan Lal[12] replied: "Progress? Swimming in the infinite ocean who is nearer the shore?"

Every human being potentially has access to the energies of the void. Our consciousness can be used like a mirror to direct the love and power of the Absolute. But we are a culture focused upon ourselves rather than on love, or the Beloved. That misdirected focus distorts and corrupts the purity of love, the creative energy of its power. Love is then no longer free and no longer brings freedom. It becomes conditioned, no longer truly creative.

In order for this energy to live its true purpose and potential, it is very important to realize that self-fulfillment, even our spiritual fulfillment, is not the center of the equation. In fact it is the very opposite of the center of the equation. The center should be kept empty. Real meaning, deep fulfillment, does not come from what happens to us. At the beginning of spiritual life this can seem a revolutionary idea, because we are conditioned to believe that our life can only be fulfilling through what happens to us.

But life flows continuously and we are part of that, just like every tree, every waterfall or butterfly. No single thing is the center of the circle whose center is everywhere. Or everything is the center; and at the center of everything is emptiness.

It has always been the emptiness at the center that allows things to happen. It has always been the hidden face of God that infuses meaning into the visible. Lao Tzu, the ancient Taoist philosopher, understood the profound functionality of the invisible:

Thirty spokes share the wheel's hub;
It is the center hole that makes it useful.
Shape clay into a vessel;

It is the space within that makes it useful.
Cut doors and windows for a room;
It is the holes that make it useful.
Therefore profit comes from what is there;
Usefulness from what is not there.[13]

The functionality of emptiness, the power of the void, is not abstract. It is not even particularly "spiritual." It is part of life at its most essential. It is an untapped energy source that belongs to life's primal nature. And yet we turn away from emptiness, from silence and stillness, and are instead caught in distraction after distraction. We don't even allow the nothingness to touch the edges of our being where it could set the imagination afire. Instead, we close those doors moment after moment, day after day, choosing a world that we imagine as solid and dependable, and wonder why life feels so much less than it could be.

NOTHINGNESS AND GRACE

When one has tasted nothingness, one accesses tremendous freedom. You return to normal consciousness knowing that you do not exist and that this world doesn't exist. Control dynamics disappear like sand through your fingers, and finally there is the joy of allowing things to happen. In the wisdom of Lao Tzu,

Less and less is done until nothing is done,
when nothing is done nothing is left undone.

There is a way to allow nothingness to benefit humanity—to give humanity breathing space, because where you don't exist you can relax. There is no struggle. Grace needs this space. And the whole of life needs what can only be given through grace.

We have so many images and stories about the relationship of emptiness and grace, though they too often sit on shelves in libraries nobody visits. This Zen *koan* tells of Subhuti, a disciple of the Buddha:

> One day, in a mood of sublime emptiness, Subhuti was resting underneath a tree when flowers began to fall about him. "We are praising you for your discourse on emptiness," the gods whispered to Subhuti. "But I have not spoken of emptiness," replied Subhuti. "You have not spoken of emptiness, we have not heard emptiness," responded the gods. "This is the true emptiness." The blossoms showered upon Subhuti as rain.[14]

And Rūmī said:

> No more words.
> In the name of this place we drink in with our
>   breathing, stay quiet like a flower.
> So the nightbirds will start singing.[15]

Through emptiness, the blossoms can fall like rain. Through silence, the song of the nightbirds rings out. In the nothingness, the heart of the world has space to spin, has silence to sing.

We know how it is in our own lives—when we live with grace, that which is hidden, mysterious, and wonderful becomes more and more part of the air we breathe. This invisible perfume is somehow always there. And the unknown, the inexpressible, is more and more present. In a strange way the invisible almost starts to veil the visible, because the intangible is so much with you, so much around you, permeating all of you.

On a true mystical path, one has lost so much. One is so lost.

In fact there comes the time when one is absorbed so completely that one's place is the placeless, one's home is the homeless.[16] Here, form and formless merge together, and one lives in the constant wonder of the created and the uncreated. Life is full and empty. This is the mystery that holds us all together. Here one can feel both presence and absence, the scent of roses and honeysuckle, and the vast, intoxicating other.

Life needs the freedom that belongs to nothingness, to what is not yet defined. Then it can be sustained by the primal energy that comes through all the levels of creation, from the Source into every moment, every grain of sand.

This energy used to be as apparent as water in a stream, but now is almost invisible. It is a primal force within creation—it *is* creation in its essence, in its most essential nature. It flows between the worlds, neither being nor nonbeing. It has an energy one could call "life," but life in its deepest sense as the energy within creation.

Nothingness can be lived—not as a threat, not as something to be afraid of. Are all the particles in our body, in matter, frightened of the space between them? No. They need the space to dance in; otherwise they can't move. Living nothingness is an affirmation of our true nature, of the space within us that is truly alive. Knowing what is formless allows us to live fully in the world of forms. And it opens a gateless gate, inviting us into the wonder of what is not, a song without words or music, a dawn without light, a night without darkness.

3

THE GIFT OF NOTHINGNESS

—◦◦◦◦◦◦—

We are the night ocean filled
With glints of light. We are the space
Between the fish and the moon,
While we sit here together.

Rūmī

We are at the end of a cycle of time. We are at a fulcrum of evolutionary change.

The signs are all around us. Perhaps the most obvious is the ecological destruction of our planet—the accelerating rate of species extinction, the drastic changes in our global climate, the vast losses of habitat, for example—all these are signs pointing towards the end of an era.

And there are other signs pointing to what is new. They are less glaring, but if we look for them we can find signs of a shift in consciousness away from a culture steeped in materialism towards values that reflect a more holistic understanding of life, or we might notice the seeds of a spiritual awakening. This shift is part of a new revelation of the Absolute, in which spiritual energies and experiences, including experiences of the void, are available in new ways.

There are dangers to this availability. Without train-ing, without guidance, human beings are likely to misun-derstand or misuse spiritual power. For example, global corporations have been the first to fully harness the aware-ness of global oneness—and to what end? To expand their spheres of exploitation, to increase the divide between rich and poor. This misuse has been allowed by humanity in part because we are not paying attention to what is being offered and what is at stake. We are still asleep, caught in our collective dreams of material prosperity.

And there are dangers to experiencing the void. Of course, in the void itself there is no danger because there is nothing there. And there is no shadow because there is nothing to reflect the light in that infinite darkness. But we do not remain in the void—we are also present in this world. An experience of the void can make it very difficult to take this world seriously, to participate in the way we are needed. But what is needed from us is to be present here, even when we know that "here" doesn't really exist. Here, at this moment, there is a work that needs to be done.

In the Bible, the parable of the laborers in the vineyard[1] provides an important teaching about the attitude required to participate in what is new, to be open to receive the divine gifts that are on offer. The parable tells of a vineyard owner who went to the market at dawn to ask for people to help him in the vineyard. He told the laborers he would pay each man a penny for his work. And they were satisfied because a penny was a good wage for the day. But then again at nine in the morning he went to the marketplace and he brought back more laborers telling them as well that he would pay them a penny at the end of the day. And when the sun was hot, at noon, he went and brought back some more laborers. And also at three in the afternoon, and again at an hour before sunset.

At the end of the day he was preparing to pay each of the laborers a penny, but those who had been working the whole day complained, saying, "These last have wrought but one hour, and thou hast made them equal unto us, which have borne the burden and heat of the day." The vineyard owner insisted he had kept his bargain and said, "I will give unto this last, even as unto thee." The parable ends with the oft-quoted saying, "So the last shall be first, and the first last: for many be called but few chosen."[2]

There is work that needs our attention, but in order to fully participate we need to step out of our ideas of how things ought to be done, of the hierarchical structures of the past. Real service means to participate freely according to the need of the moment without counting the hours or days, or who did more than who. It asks that we be present both in the world of time and space—"the burden and heat of the day"—and the freedom that comes from the inner worlds, where time opens out into the eternal and the Real comes into life.[3]

THE POWER OF ATTENTION

In order to work with the energy of the Absolute on any level, we need the right attitude, attention, and intention. When it comes to the void and the hidden substance of God we need to remember that attention does not need *something* as an object. Rather, attention is a receptive state of being.

In Sufism, attention is subtly linked to intention, which is an attitude of mind, an attitude of being, that carries with it a whole mystical tradition of *ādāb*. *Ādāb* refers to "courtesy of behavior." From a superficial view, *ādāb* might look like simple politeness or a prescribed way of acting. But in fact, *ādāb* is based on the relationship between the soul and God—the way the soul is before God. Over time, this fundamental inner relationship that includes humility, respect, devotion, and continual watchfulness becomes part of our daily pattern of behavior—our way of interacting with life, with each other, with the path, and with the Absolute.

The Sufis say life is the greatest teacher. So while there is respect for one's individual teacher or guru, there is also great respect towards life, respect towards one's self, and the deep knowing that everything is God.

In Sufi stories this state of awareness is described by the image of a cat at the mouse hole. The cat is infinitely attentive, infinitely relaxed, in a state of watchful receptivity.

Meditation can be a foundation for this kind of attention, but there is a danger in making what is a fundamental capacity of the Self a special "practice." The contemporary Tibetan Buddhist Rinpoche Namkhai Norbu tells a story about a 13th-century Dzogchen master:

> The great Dzogchen master, Yungton Dorje Pal, was asked:
> "What meditation do you do?" And he replied: "What would I meditate on?"
> So his questioner concluded: "In Dzogchen you don't meditate, then?"
> But Yungton Dorje Pal replied: "When am I ever distracted?"[4]

In Sufism there is a story of Bāyezīd Bistāmī, who was sitting at the feet of his teacher when this exchange took place:

"Bāyezīd, fetch me that book from the window!" the master said.

"The window? Which window?" asked Bāyezīd.

"Why," said the master, "you have been coming here all this time and didn't see the window?"

"No," replied Bāyezīd. "What have I to do with the window? When I am before you I close my eyes to everything else. I have not come to stare about."

"Since that is so," said the teacher, "go back to Bistām. Your work is completed."

Attention has to do with the practice of witnessing, described in the *Mundaka Upanishad* through the story of the two birds sitting on a branch of a tree. One bird eats the sweet fruit of the tree while the other bird looks on, without eating. This mysterious passage describes the aspect of ourselves involved in life and the aspect that seems not to be—the part that simply watches. Spiritual practices like meditation help awaken this "witness," what the Sufis call the *shāhid*. Eternal and present, and not restricted by cause and effect, it is an aspect of the Self or soul.

Witnessing is not an abstraction from life, but rather a multi-dimensional participation, a way to be of service. Through witnessing, we are not focused on accomplishing something, gaining something, realizing or learning something; rather, we are attentive and available. We are fully present without desire or need.

At its deepest, this quality of attention participates in the remembrance of the Divine on all levels. Ibn 'Arabī calls the mystic "the pupil in the eye of humanity,"[5] through which God sees His own world. Without human consciousness, especially the awakened consciousness of the heart, the Absolute is not known, does not know Itself. This is reflected in the primordial covenant, when the soul of the not-yet-created humanity was asked, "Am I not your Lord?" and they replied, "Yes, we witness it."[6] We aspire to remember and live the soul's covenant.

Witnessing encompasses both presence and absence, for it cannot take place solely from within creation. If the witness were solely in the created world, the witnessing would be veiled by creation. It would be like the bird focused only on the sweet fruit. Rather, part of the witness remains outside of creation—the second bird that "looks on." From behind the veils of creation, it can see and know the Real throughout all levels of reality.

In Sufi esoteric science the different spiritual centers within the heart embrace different levels of reality, and these centers, or "chambers of the heart," each carry a unique spiritual consciousness. Each center of consciousness witnesses a different level of reality—from the outer chamber, *Qalb*, that awakens us to our longing for God; to the inner chamber of *Khafī*, that witnesses the dark light of the primal nothingness of non-existence; and then beyond into the innermost chamber that experiences only Absolute Truth.[7] Witnessing is a way of remembering the Real, and reminding the Real of its own divinity, that it is "Lord."

At certain times this quality of inner and outer attention needs to become more active. Something in one's life will call us to be awake in a new way. This call will be different for different people. It likely will not be what we expect, what we are hoping for, what we want. Something at work, something in an ordinary day, or a thought or hint of something … an insight in meditation, maybe even a scent in the air or a gust of wind across a field. Something in life has a need for one's conscious attention—it might last a few seconds, or a week, or even a year.

In these moments if one responds with the right attitude, the right intention, then one experiences a quality of awakeness that is both present and absent. One becomes a doorway. Something can be born into life that wasn't there before; an aspect of the Absolute can come alive for the first time.

In the Sufi tradition this moment is imaged in the story of when Moses met Khidr—"one of Our servants whom We have given mercy and bestowed knowledge of Ourself."[8] In the story, Moses wants to meet with Khidr and is told that Khidr can be found at the place where the two seas meet. He is also told that a sign of Khidr's presence is that in this place "the cooked fish becomes alive again."

So Moses and his companion search but do not find Khidr. Only when they stop for their morning meal, hungry from the journey, and discover that their cooked fish has swum off into the water, does Moses realize that they have passed the place where Khidr was without noticing. They have to retrace their steps.

It is part of spiritual training to be present and watchful, prepared for these moments where the worlds come together, where the two seas meet and the dead fish comes alive.[9] The spiritual path teaches us to live in a state of attention, with one foot in the uncreated world and one in creation, so that when these moments come we will notice, and will be free to respond with what is needed where it is needed.

These moments can be opportunities related to our own spiritual growth, or they might have nothing to do with us. But if one catches these moments when the levels of reality are aligned, when the doors of grace are opening, when all one has to do is pay attention and be willing to follow, then the whole of life—inner and outer—can change.

In the late 1950s, the Chilean writer Miguel Serrano went on a pilgrimage in India in search of truth. On his way to Benares he visited the Sufi master Radha Mohan Lal in Kanpur. He describes how the Sufi master would walk in his garden in the evening, carrying his rosary, praying. One evening the Sufi master called Miguel to him and sang him a tender story of a shepherd who was looking for Krishna, and who, after passing through many valleys and over mountain passes, one day entered a house, asking for food. At that very moment Krishna himself passed along the road. Later on the shepherd heard how he had missed the encounter, and he uttered this sad lament: "I have lost my heart along the way and never found it again."[10]

The shepherd never met Krishna, because at that moment he was not present, he was not attentive. He was in a house asking for food. Without his full attention, the planes could not meet, could not interact. The shepherd's life did not change. The search continued. If his attention had been correct, the planes of reality could have aligned and his life would have changed forever.

And Miguel Serrano continued on his journey as well.

Such moments come in our individual lives as well as in our collective lives—times when forces in the inner and outer worlds are aligning to support change, moments that require our full watchfulness and attention. As Shakespeare writes in *Julius Caesar,*

> There is a tide in the affairs of men,
> Which, taken at the flood, leads on to fortune;
> Omitted, all the voyage of their life
> Is bound in shallows and in miseries.[11]

At this moment in our global history the tide in the affairs of men is turning. This turning,[12] this evolutionary moment, needs our full attention. We can remember how to watch; we can remember how to catch these moments, how to see beneath the surface. Nothingness helps us be attentive. With one foot in nothingness, with one ear attuned to silence, we are infinitely watchful and undisturbed.

THE DANGERS OF NOTHINGNESS

We cannot be attentive to the moment if we are too engaged with life. But at the same time, we cannot be attentive to the moment if we escape into the inner worlds or into the void.

It requires a great deal of spiritual maturity to work with the uncreated while respecting the world of existence. It can take many years to fully accept life here, in this world, with all of its limitations, distortions, and often needless suffering. This is particularly true when you have glimpsed the inner reality of light upon light, or experienced

the emptiness, and felt the outer world become less sub-
stantial, holding less and less interest or attraction for you.
These experiences can bring anger, frustration, bitterness,
and even a certain psycho-spiritual neurosis, which drives
a compulsion to deny life's outer reality.

But denial is not spiritual maturity. We can remember
the story of the Zen student who, when he declared to
his teacher that all life is an illusion, was hit hard by the
teacher's stick. When the student shouted in pain, his
teacher responded, "Was that an illusion?"

Experiences of nothingness can bring tremendous
disappointment in their wake. We step on the path because
we are missing something, we long for something, we need
something. We might be told that we will not get anything,
that the path is not about us, and yet we are convinced
our lives will be made better and *we* will be made better
through spiritual practice. Enlightenment, nirvana, para-
dise, heaven—whatever it is, it is always *something*.

On a real mystical path, the teacher prepares the
student for a gradual awareness, a gradual awakening to
nothingness. For a long time the student is terrified to take
this leap into oblivion, to fall into the abyss of eternity. But
when the letting go happens, one realizes that one hasn't
fallen anywhere because there's nowhere to fall. The idea
of falling into the abyss belongs to the concept of existence.
This was well described by the 9th-century Chan Buddhist
master, Huang Po:

Ordinary people look to their surroundings, while
followers of the Way look to Mind, but the true
Dharma is to forget them both. The former is easy

enough, the latter very difficult. Men are afraid to forget their minds, fearing to fall through the Void with nothing to stay their fall. They do not know that the Void is not really void, but the realm of the real Dharma.[13]

If we are lucky, the experience of non-being will set us free and help us laugh at the joke of existence—the great secret that what we have searched for does not exist and at the same time is everywhere. The joke is on us. There is always laughter if we allow ourselves to be laughed at. This current of laughter ripples through everything, and laughing at ourselves, we become part of life's wonderful, love-filled, ecstatic joke.

But one does not just disappear into the joke. One lives it. It is important to understand that there needs to be somebody to get the joke; otherwise there is nobody to laugh.

This is part of the great hidden meaning of being human—we are here to participate in all levels of reality. We need to celebrate the emptiness of reality, not use it as a way to deny what is. If we are caught in patterns of denial, disappointment, anger, then the Real remains unrecognized, uncelebrated.

In the West we do not have many teachings that explain how to live with the awareness of non-being, to exist and non-exist at the same time. Yet, Sufism has a detailed understanding of the states of non-existence—what is referred to as "abiding after passing away." A famous saying of Kharaqānī, alluded to by Rūmī, suggests that non-existence is the very nature of the Sufi dervish:

There is no dervish in the world, and if there
were a dervish, this would not be a dervish.[14]

Real existence, life as divine, can only be experienced
through non-existence, through annihilation. But ultimately this does not mean that we turn away from the
world. Rather, we learn to respect the world and its limitations. We learn to walk in both worlds.

We also come to understand that there are consequences to not taking this world seriously, even though we
know its illusory nature. One can actually impede one's
spiritual work and miss opportunities by not acknowledging the rules of this world.

In the Gospel of St. Matthew (22:15), Jesus is asked by his
disciples about paying taxes to the Roman government. Jesus
asks his disciples to give him a penny, and says, "Whose is
this image and subscription?" They said unto him, "Caesar's."
And he said, "Render therefore unto Caesar the things that
are Caesar's and unto God the things that are God's."

There are very strict rules governing how energies
work on each plane of reality and how one can work with
them. This Biblical passage is a profound teaching pointing
to the need to honor different levels of reality with what
is appropriate to each level, not to mix levels, and not to
ignore one level in preference for another.

It is in this ordinary world, where the Absolute is
veiled, that humanity participates in the unveiling, in the
revelation. In this divine love affair of creation—the dance
of the Beloved—the lover has a part to play. But if we seek
to escape this world after a taste of inner bliss or nothingness, we cannot fully participate. We stop watching,
we stop paying attention; we stop being available.

Instead of escaping life, the mystic surrenders into life, awake on different levels of reality, attending to each as needed.

ORDINARY LIFE

The ground of nothingness is ordinary life. "Chop wood, carry water" is a way of living that allows life to be itself and frees the different levels of reality from our spiritual projections, our expectations and disappointments.

Householder traditions have long pointed to the importance of accepting our own humanness and the imperfections of life. In Sufism, there are two kinds of retreat. One is the outward kind in which the seeker, far from people, sits alone in his cell until he comes into contact with the spiritual world. This result comes about because the external senses withdraw themselves and the inner senses extend themselves to signs from the spiritual world.

The second kind of retreat is the hidden one, where the seeker is inwardly witnessing the secrets of the Real while she is outwardly surrounded by people. This is the Naqshbandi Sufi principle[15] of *Solitude in the Crowd* (*Khalwat dar anjuman*), which means "outwardly to be with the people, inwardly to be with God." This principle supports the mystic while she engages with both the outer and the inner world, balancing and bridging them.

The more one is absorbed into nothingness the more important it is to remain grounded in outer life. In fact much of the mundanity of a mystical path has a deep purpose. In the Naqshbandi tradition it is the correct combination of the inner secrets with the most ordinary things that

makes possible the mystical journey. In the words of
Khwāja Faghnawī, "our science is not of the world, it is of
the worlds."[16] It is this immersion in ordinariness, com-
bined with the awareness of what is beyond the physical
world, that allows a certain key to be turned, a certain lock
to be opened.

When one has been fully immersed in nothingness,
some part of oneself never comes back. It is tremendously
powerful to be here and there, in being and non-being both.
This human capacity to become a nexus of the inner and
outer, of not-being and being, of what is written and what
is not yet written, is key to aligning the worlds and keeping
life in balance. Life was made to function not as just the
outer plane of reality, but as a multidimensional, interre-
lating reality. And there need to be those who know this
secret.

The Sufi teacher Irina Tweedie used to tell her students
a story about a four-legged chicken. The story goes that a
man was driving down a country lane and spotted a four-
legged chicken running very, very fast along the road.
Fascinated, he followed the chicken and came to a farmyard
where he asked the farmer if he had seen that remarkable
sight! The farmer explained that he had. In fact, he had
bred the four-legged chicken because he and his family—
his wife and two children—all liked to eat the legs of a
chicken. He thought, with this special breed, everyone in
the family could eat what they wanted. The traveler was
impressed, and asked the farmer how the chicken tasted.
The farmer threw up his hands and explained, "I don't
know! We've never caught it!"

This odd and ironic little story is really a very accurate
description of what it is like for the seeker on a spiritual

path. Through spiritual practices, if they are effective, one creates a spiritual vehicle—a way for one's consciousness to function on the different levels of reality. This spiritual vehicle spins at a higher frequency than the ego and the ordinary mind. So the seeker never catches up, never really has access to these other aspects of herself. This doesn't mean that her vehicle is not functioning. In fact, the vehicle functions best without the interference of the ego, without the ordinary consciousness getting in the way or trying to control it.

Unfortunately, it is almost inconceivable for most Western spiritual seekers to accept that they will not get something from their hard work, that the benefits of their practices do not belong to them. Our culture is so extremely self-focused that we have corrupted, without realizing it, many of our spiritual intentions and efforts by trying to control, co-opt, and benefit from something that does not belong to us—that never belonged to us, but has always belonged to the Real.

While some teachings and traditions acknowledge the need for the extinction of the individual self, which is central to classical Sufism (the absence of the dervish that Rūmī celebrates), the methods of reaching this state are rarely available.[17] The practices have been diluted or corrupted and instead of being given access to the level of the Self and its world of light upon light, or beyond, into the primal emptiness, the seeker too often remains stranded in the illusory nature of the outer world, or a spiritual illusion created by the ego. The spiritual ideal of "ordinary life" does not then include a mature balance of the inner and outer.

There is a great need to acknowledge and accept how spiritual life functions, to understand "the science of the worlds." Ordinary life can then ground the "extraordinary" —the secrets of the inner to which spiritual practices give us access. This "grounding" does not always mean we have synchronicities in our life, or that we meet a soul mate, or that we become healthy—some of the goals and assurances of our contemporary spiritual collective. It means the Real has a place to be, with us and through us. And we might never know what that means.

Our acceptance of the ordinary is part of our spiritual maturity and capacity to be of service. It also helps us to avoid the trap of inflation, which can easily catch us when we glimpse a world beyond the ego. It is only too easy to identify with an inner experience.[18] But when we let go of wanting spiritual life to be about us, when we live in the various dimensions without mixing the levels or imposing expectations and desires, this freedom allows us to fully participate in spiritual work.

Present in both the inner and outer world, one learns to serve the world, serve life, serve others without effort. This is a very careful balance. If one takes upon oneself the onerous responsibility of service, then the ego easily gets caught in it; the psyche gets encumbered by it. But being engaged in an ordinary life allows us to be of service without the burden of thinking we can solve the world's or other people's problems, which brings with it self-importance and, worse, spiritual self-importance.

Naqshbandi Sufis have always lived this way, forsaking special robes and working in ordinary jobs, traditionally often as craftsmen—Bahā ad-Dīn Naqshband was a potter, 'Attār a perfumer. And of course many of the great Zen and Taoist teachers emphasized the ordinary and the dangers of spiritual importance:

Emperor Wu: "I have built many temples, copied innumerable Sutras and ordained many monks since becoming Emperor. Therefore, I ask you, what is my merit?"

Bodhidharma: "None whatsoever!"

Emperor Wu: "Why no merit?"

Bodhidharma: "Doing things for merit has an impure motive and will only bear the puny fruit of rebirth."

Emperor Wu, a little put out: "What then is the most important principle of Buddhism?"

Bodhidharma: "Vast emptiness. Nothing sacred."

Emperor Wu, by now bewildered, and not a little indignant: "Who is this that stands before me?"

Bodhidharma: "I do not know."

If we can allow ourselves to live an ordinary life while also staying awake to the great void at the center of all that is, then we can be this intermediary place between that intoxicating, mystical bliss of oblivion and the wonder of how the Divine creates and reveals Itself in all the forms of life. Our lives are the expression of this bridge—ordinary and extraordinary, all things in their place, everything free to be as it is, and our consciousness, our heart, free to be used as needed.

Certain things of this world are more real than others, and only through this unique state that is both here and not here can we find them—can we be attentive and care for them. It is a strange spiritual game, like finding Easter eggs as a child. There are signs pointing to where they are, but you can't see the signs if your eyes are blinkered, caught in either worldly or spiritual concepts. But if you have even just for a moment been immersed in nothingness, and if you are willing to live that awareness here in daily life, then you can be used in this game of revelation, the hide-and-seek of the Real.

Our participation, our willingness to serve, is a living acknowledgment that we are not separate from God. How can we be separate from that which is indivisible? Annihilation, *fanā*, frees us from ignorance, awakening us to an awareness of our oneness with God. Within this oneness there is work to be done, and those who are both here and not here, both present and absent, can do that work.

Mystics have gone beyond the clouds to the sky, gone beyond the sky to the spaces between the stars, into the dazzling darkness where the names of God are in potential. And yet we are also here, with our feet on the ground, breathing into life those names, so that the stories of divine love can be written in both worlds.

4

ONENESS

—◦⟆⟅◦—

In that abyss I saw how love held bound
Into one volume all the leaves whose flight
Is scattered through the universe around.

Dante[1]

Between existence and non-existence, between creation
and the void, is a thread that connects the worlds. It neither
exists nor does not exist.

This thread is spun with the light of oneness. It is made
of love and woven into the central chamber of the human
heart, the seat of the Self. The *Katha Upanishad* describes the
Self as "that boundless Power, source of every power,
manifesting itself as life, entering every heart."[2]

On the plane of the Self all is One. Through the consciousness of the Self, what the Sufis call "the eye of the
heart," a human being experiences the oneness of life: all
of life as a single dynamic interconnected web in which all
levels of existence and nonexistence interpenetrate each
other. This consciousness of the Self, or Mind as it is expressed in Dzogchen Buddhism, is a consciousness of
Oneness:

Mind of mine, dwelling in the present
Uncontrived, uncoarsened, and untouched
Heart essence of all that is,
Dwells solely as wholeness unbounded.[3]

In the void, the oneness of the Absolute has yet to be revealed. As life's primal substance flows from non-being into being, from emptiness into form, it moves through a single point that contains the existence of the whole in potential.

From this point, life explodes into multiplicity, into the wonder and majesty of creation's almost infinite variety. This is the "big bang" of modern physics, but it is not something that happened just once in a distant past. Rather, this birth is continuous, unceasing—a moment-by-moment happening. Through our awareness we catch this moment, both transient and eternal, as simple as spring's blossoming, as described by the Zen master Dogen:

Emptiness is bound to bloom, like hundreds of grasses blossoming. Although originally having no flowers, it now has flowers. It is, as it were, a plum tree that some days ago did not have flowers but blooms when spring arrives. It is the time of flowers, and flowers have arrived ... The flowering of plums and willows happens to plums and willows; that of peaches and damsons to peaches and damsons. The way the flowers of emptiness [*kuge*, literally "sky-flowers," the illusory forms of the relative world] open is also like this.[4]

Through our awareness we catch this moment, both transient and eternal; we are present at this point where form is born out of emptiness, this moment of blossoming. Our awakened awareness serves the Absolute by recognizing the true nature of the relative—that it is One.

Just as we can recognize the void as part of the multi-dimensional reality in which we live, so too can we know and live the oneness of the Absolute, the dimension of the Self, or soul. And just as there are ways to work with the energies of the void, there are ways to work with the energies of oneness, which include a freedom that is independent of power dynamics, a love that flows where it is needed, and a unifying presence beyond any duality.

One cannot do this work without the attitude of service. And this attitude or state of servanthood comes not from a place of being separate from the Absolute, but from a place of being one with It. "Union is the very secret of servanthood," said Ibn 'Arabī.[5] Through the real nature of service we live from a place of oneness even if initially we are not fully conscious of it. In time, with grace, awareness of unity dawns. The boundaries of separation and duality dissolve in the energy of love and the light of oneness:

> My servant ceases not to draw nigh unto Me by works of devotion, until I love him, and when I love him I am the eye by which he sees and the ear by which he hears.[6]

Collectively, we don't understand the esoteric reality of interdependence. We see connectedness on the physical plane and are becoming more aware of ecological interdependence. But we are not generally aware of how different levels of reality interpenetrate, or how our attitude and consciousness can create inner barriers. For example, our mental concept of separation and our Western focus on the individual ego-self have created an isolating field of consciousness. Its density and constriction block the way light and energy can flow throughout the whole, including the physical. This drains light and life force (*prana* in Sanskrit) from the body and the soul of the world, depleting the Earth of its vitality both physically and spiritually.

This happens on an individual level—both the body and soul of a human being can lose their energy and light if an individual thinks and acts in such a way that cuts him or her off from what is real and sustaining. So too can the world lose its light, for the whole is not separate from us. Being of service requires an attitude and state of consciousness that recognize the inherent oneness throughout creation, a deep knowing that we are not separate but part of a living whole that exists both within and around us. We need to recognize that our consciousness as well as our actions affect life as a whole.

Many have glimpsed oneness, seen "a world in a grain of sand, and a heaven in a wild flower."[7] And through spiritual practice, seekers throughout time have sought to live and more deeply experience this awareness. But the light of oneness is available to all of us, present in hidden aquifers where life's waters continue to flow, waiting in a living silence for us to notice.

SILENCE

However constricted in the outer world, the energies of oneness are alive in silence—in the silence underneath every sound, present in the space around every atom—a silence saturated with the Real.

Silence is singing with love. There is love that exists in forms, sounds, and activities—we feel its presence in beauty, are touched by its joy. But there is also love present in emptiness, in silence, in space—a love that does not require recognition, that just is. The mystic is absorbed by this love that at once takes her into the infinite and grounds her in the web of life, for silence is an open passageway between the worlds.

Through spiritual practices like meditation or watching the breath, mystics become familiar with this silence. It happens quite naturally that we dwell in silence, for silence pervades the depths into which the mystic dives again and again. This silence is undefined and speaks to us of the undefined vistas of our own being, and the greater mystery that pervades everything.

Even when the mind is busy, one becomes aware that underneath the activity of the mind there is stillness. One becomes more and more present, resting there, so the silence becomes the hidden foundation of life. Rūmī wrote of this silence:

> Out beyond ideas of wrongdoing and rightdoing,
> there is a field. I'll meet you there.
>
> When the soul lies down in that grass,
> the world is too full to talk about.[8]

And Bāyezīd Bistāmī:

> All this talk and turmoil and noise and movement
> is outside the veil. Inside the veil is silence and
> calm and peace.

Mystical practices belong to what is inside the veil, to this underlying silence present everywhere. Mystical practices often work without our knowing it—they enter the unconscious, into the bloodstream where they transform us. They take us back to the root of our existence, back to the oneness where we belong with God, where His name is our name.

The silence of the Real is not personal. It is vaster and deeper than your sense of your self. It is not interested in your troubles; it will likely not make you feel like a better person. It may not make you feel more integrated, wise, or whatever it is most of us think spiritual life is about. In fact, it isn't interested in us, individually. It often leaves the ego-structure quite intact. But it is at work in the deepest parts of life, forging its way through barriers, permeating the velvet darkness of the mystical night, echoing with love throughout the whole of creation.

Part of the Naqshbandi Sufi practice is to learn to be always present in this silence. This is one of the foundations of the path. Bahā ad-Dīn Naqshband said, "God is silent and is most easily reached in silence." The silent *dhikr*, the silent repetition of the name of God, is a central Naqshbandi practice.[9] It was given to 'Abd'l-Khāliq Ghijduwānī by Khidr who, in a vision or dream, submerged him under water and then told him: *Now, repeat the name of God.*

This dimension of silence where the Real is present is so simple. It is very beautiful, and it is very powerful because here there are no distortions caused by noise. Of course all the noise and the multitude of sounds are part of life. Life is made up of this multiplicity. It is part of the play of creation that we become lost in the ten-thousand things and the oneness that is our real nature is scattered—until finally in those ten-thousand things we discover once again the oneness, and we return to the oneness that we have in truth never left.

The mystic comes to accept that the One is known through the many. And yet if we are inwardly immersed in the silence it is easier not to get scattered, easier for our consciousness to rest in the primal oneness of life.

Working with oneness requires the attention described in the previous chapter—an attention that is always listening, always watchful. But unlike the void, oneness can be heard, seen, felt, tasted. In it we find a wholeness that nourishes and connects, a love that embraces all life as sacred, a beauty that weaves the worlds together, and a way of living that expands to include all experience—both the dark and light. In the light of oneness, suffering and darkness are accepted as part of life, part of the inexplicable that embraces us.

In oneness, we can find a love that has no prejudice, but embraces life and draws the various aspects of life together. It is an invisible love, not limited by form, but fully present nonetheless. Mystics love the invisible. In Sufism, the seeker longs for a hidden Beloved, loves the silence, and gives herself to a teacher who knows non-existence, who is absorbed in nothingness. Through our love for the invisible, the mystic infuses love with the void, and brings the fullness of the void into life. It was always meant to be this way.

Great power and love are waiting in this silence, waiting to be called through the emptiness, through the stillness, into life. Just through being present we participate, through being aware we are in service—a presence and awareness that are not scattered, not lost in forgetfulness. This is about being rather than doing, mindful of the simple essence of life, what is most precious and yet all around us:

Sitting silently
Doing nothing
Spring comes
And the grass grows by itself.[10]

THE BREATH

Human beings are microcosms of the whole. The Source births the one, the two, and the ten-thousand things that turn our attention back to the One: "In everything there is a witness that points to the fact that He is one."[11] This cycle of birth and death, expression and absorption, takes place within us with every cycle of the breath.

Each breath is an invitation into the oneness of the Absolute. Each breath connects all levels of reality, the inner and the outer. Through the breath, heaven and earth unite.

The breath belongs to the esoteric core of much spiritual work and the processes of inner transformation. Just as breathing is fundamental to many forms of life, breath and the awareness of the breath are central to many spiritual practices, whether it is the simple meditation practice of watching your breath, or repeating a *mantra* or *dhikr*. The Buddha gave particular emphasis to the breath:

One who has gradually practiced,
Developed and brought to perfection
Mindfulness of the in-and-out breath
As taught by the Enlightened One,
Illuminates the entire world
Like the moon when freed from clouds.[12]

Both Sufism and Buddhism emphasize the space between the breaths. Bahā ad-Dīn Naqshband said: "The foundation of our work is in the breath. The more that one is able to be conscious of one's breathing, the stronger is one's inner life. It is a must for everyone to safeguard his breath in the time of his inhalation and exhalation and further, to safeguard his breath in the interval between the inhalation and exhalation."[13] And in an ancient Sanskrit text that echoes the roots of Zen, it is written, "As breath turns from down to up, and again as breath curves from up to down—through both these turns, *realize*."[14]

Why is this moment between the breaths so important, so meaningful? With each in-breath we return from the physical world to the inner plane of the Self. If one is very attentive one can experience an instant of bliss at the end of the in-breath, which is a momentary experience of bliss of the Self, known in Sanskrit as *anandamaya kosha* (the sheath of the soul). In this experience of Self, no matter how brief, we are free from time, awake in the timeless realm of the soul, in the bliss and peace that is our real nature.[15]

The awakening of the Self is an awakening to an all-embracing oneness, which is at first intoxicating and awe-inspiring, and yet completely natural. Resting in the Self we rest in this oneness. It is a state of being. Often an initial experience of the Self is a state of presence, or *pure being*, the simple wonder of being human. We know we *are*, part of a reality beyond duality, beyond this world of opposites. And when we fully awaken in the Self we experience a pure consciousness that is non-dual. It *is*. It *knows*. There is no subject or object—only oneness. The pure consciousness of the awakened Self is the light of oneness.

This consciousness has no judgment. It is compassion, complete acceptance and pure love. When we discover our Self we discover that we are one with our Self and one with everything. In us everything is united, everything is whole. This is the circle of wholeness that belongs to all of life, in which all of life is sacred. Nothing is excluded. The Self is the multifaceted diamond, the mandala that unites all aspects of experience, even seemingly opposing elements. "All differences in this world are of degree, and not of kind, because oneness is the secret of everything," said Vivekananda.

Every in-breath gives us access to the energies of the Self, the light and consciousness of oneness. Most people are unconsciously pursuing the experiences of the Self— the energies of oneness—in their longing for love, their search for meaning and belonging, their yearning to be met and truly known. The traditional spiritual journey is simply a more conscious and intentional commitment to this fundamental human need, as the seeker turns away from the world to find the Real. Through practices of the path, through deep meditation, and with the grace of the teacher, the mystic makes the return journey beyond the ego. Gradually, the veils of separation begin to lift to reveal the Self that is the breath of all.

And of course the mystical path takes us even further, beyond the Self into the emptiness, beyond its dazzling light into the dazzling darkness, beyond the state of being into non-being and the uncreated emptiness.

But there is no in-breath without the out-breath, the outpouring from the Source into all the forms of life, the nourishing of the outer planes with the energies of the inner.

The journey of the out-breath has not been historically emphasized. Instead, we have images of the monk sitting in deep meditation, the *sadhu* wandering the hills in his rags of renunciation, lost forever to the outer, ordinary world.

Now there is a need for humanity to breathe back into life the sustaining energies of the Self, to consciously ignite the soul of the world with the light of our own soul by knowing they are one. Through the mystery of the out-breath, the sustaining energies of the Source can revitalize the outer world of forms. Just as we are continually sustained by the energy of the Self, so is the world sustained by the energy of the Real that comes from the inner planes.

The more our awareness is grounded in the Self, awake to oneness—rather than constricted by the separateness of our ego—the more we experience and share this sustenance. In fact our awareness enables the Self to participate more directly in our life: through our conscious alignment with the Real, It comes into our life or reveals Itself in our life.

This is the significance of spiritual practices designed to transform or purify the lower nature, what the Sufi calls *polishing the mirror of the heart*. Having traveled the path, having cleaned the inner mirror, the mystic clearly sees the Real all around: "wheresoever you turn, there is the face of God."[16]

This inner work of polishing enables the light of the real sun to be reflected into our life. This light nourishes both our own life and life around us. This has traditionally been part of the work of the mystic: to bring the pure light of the Self into her immediate surroundings, making a real contribution to the inner and outer environment. Through the silent devotion of the heart, the sweetness of remembrance comes into this world of forgetfulness.

But we don't need this polishing to be complete in order to reflect the light of oneness into life. Polishing can be a lifetime's work, and the world is calling out for remembrance *now*. Remembrance can be a moment-to-moment experience, when for an instant the veils lift and we are fully present. The awareness of the breath brings us back to this present moment, a moment in which we live the cycle of creation that goes from the formless into form and then back to the formless. We experience the pure emptiness of what is formless, at the end of the in-breath, "ah"—when we go back to that moment of bliss, between the in-breath and the out-breath. Then the breath returns us, back into the physical world.

This is the whole cycle of life, in which at that moment we are fully present, both as witness and co-creator. We are fully alive in the place where the two seas meet, where form and the formless come together.

> In the beginning there was nothing,
>   nor was anything lacking.
> The paper was blank. We pick up the
>   paint brush and create the scene ...
> The landscape, the wind whipping water
>   in waves.

Everything depends upon the stroke
    of our brush.
Our Ox lets the good earth lead it,
Just as our brush allows our hand to move it.
Take any direction, roam the world to
    its farthest edge.
All comes back to where it started ...
    to blessed Emptiness.

Hsu Yun[17]

EVOLVING ONENESS

The moment-to-moment cycle of life, the dance between the One and the many, is not fixed. Like all aspects of the Absolute, oneness evolves. Within oneness there is a consciousness, a light, that determines the patterns of manifestation, that guides the ways the many reflect the One. If humanity can learn to work with this light, to participate in how the energies of oneness manifest in the world, then so much change is possible.

Those individuals committed to spiritual life, stabilized on the plane of oneness, are not enough to renew the dying world we live in. There is a deep need for the energy of oneness to be given to the whole of life, to nourish and transform it. There is spiritual work to be done by those who have not yet completed the journey Home, who have been given a glimpse of their real nature but still remain in the ego.

All that is needed is that we recognize the larger dimension of spiritual work and no longer focus on our individual inner journey or our own spiritual well-being.

We live the whole cycle of the breath—understanding that the whole of life needs renewal, and we are willing to be used for this purpose, to be of service in this way.

This shift is not so easy for seekers who have identified spiritual work solely with the image of self-development, or the individual journey Home. But our world is crying out for the energy of the Real. Our spiritual journey is part of the Earth's journey, our breath is the breath of life. Spiritual life is about a wholeness that includes all of creation. The light of oneness can banish the illusion of separation and help humanity to see the web of life of which we are a part.

When we bring this awareness of oneness into life we help life to awaken to its true nature, as a self-sustaining organism that has its own spiritual consciousness. We recognize and support the natural flow of resources—inner and outer—through the web of existence, and unblock the constrictions that allow resources to be hoarded by the few. This is not a naïve spiritual dream, but rather it is what is possible when human beings live what is given.

One of the most pressing needs of our time is to unify the seeming opposites of spirit and matter. The light of oneness ignites the magic inherent in matter, releases the spiritual potential of matter and the beneficial forces within creation. The loss of this magic is part of the esoteric desolation of the Earth, why creation is losing its light. Human beings have played a key role in this desolation. Just as we have forgotten the names of creation, we have separated ourselves from the whole of creation—we have, as Thomas Berry puts it, "broken the great conversation" with the natural world:

We are talking only to ourselves. We are not talking to the rivers, we are not listening to the wind
and stars. We have broken the great conversation.
By breaking that conversation we have shattered
the universe. All the disasters that are happening
now are a consequence of that spiritual "autism."[18]

Our spiritual journey is part of the Earth's journey, the
journey of the rivers and the wind and the stars, the seeds
and the rain. Life needs the power of this primal magic to
help it evolve, and it needs the light of oneness to reignite
it. Otherwise, life will remain stagnant, humanity will continue to go round and round in cycles of increasing darkness
and destruction.

Human beings are powerful transformers of energy.
Each human being contains the whole. Through our spiritual centers we are connected to the spiritual energies of
the inner worlds that sustain us, as well as to the ancient
energies of the Earth. Accessing these energies is so simple,
requiring only that we turn to the part of ourselves that is
already attuned to the whole—to that feeling in our heart
and soul that life needs our help. We do not always need
to do something to "help." We just need to allow our sense
of connection, our growing compassion, our feelings of
responsibility, to sustain and direct us. We learn to listen
and to be present in our listening.

We will respond individually, but specifically there is
a need to bring together higher and lower energies through
groups. Spiritual groups have traditionally been used to
ground energies from the higher planes and can do so
more quickly and channel more energy than individuals.
Groups of people who pray and meditate together, whose

consciousness is attuned to one another, and to the Divine, are exponentially more powerful than individuals.

Traditionally, it has been a secret that spiritual groups can be used to focus energy from the inner planes into creation. A spiritual group that is bonded together is a very powerful organism of light, and can be used as a lens that brings higher energies into life. The more inwardly aligned the group is, the higher the frequency that can be transmitted. The energy can then be directed where it is needed. Just as one can direct one's attention anywhere in the physical body, energy can be directed anywhere into the body of humanity.[19] And as these groups are linked together in the inner and outer worlds, they form a web of light around the globe that is designed to help humanity and the Earth make a shift in our shared evolution.[20]

But sadly, many spiritual groups are as caught in images of separation as the collective, are too focused on the individual and its image of spiritual life, or imprisoned in hierarchical structures. Many groups still emphasize personal transformation or self-empowerment, rather than understanding the deeper need to be in relationship to the whole; while some groups may emphasize how they are different, even superior to other spiritual groups, rather than recognizing how each living spiritual tradition is one note in a symphony of light.[21] Life's organic energy cannot flow through these structures; they restrict the light of Divine Oneness. These groups are unable to participate in this work.

Whether we are working within ourselves or in a group, our participation is needed for the whole of life to evolve. Only the Divine can change and heal the world; only the energy and power of the Real can free the world from its self-destructive illusions. But this energy and awareness of the Real is within each of us, *is* each of us. When we turn away from the ego and its desires, we come to know that we are the Real, and because we contain the whole within us, that consciousness can awaken the light within life.

If we can be present in the silence, between the in-breath and the out-breath, holding the connection between our soul and the soul of the world, our body and the body of the Earth, then magic can happen—the real magic that belongs to the Creator and the creation. This is magic that has not been contaminated by the past or constricted by our collective thought-forms, but belongs to the nature of life itself.

The very foundation of life is miraculous, and contains this magic waiting to happen. It can help to heal and restore what we have polluted and desecrated. It allows for real sustainability, for the rains to come and the crops to grow, and can enable us once again to listen to the Earth as a living whole—to care for the soul as well as the soil. We are this place where the worlds come together, where the consciousness of life's oneness can reawaken.

In the dynamic interconnected whole, we carry the awareness of the in-breath that draws all existence back to the Absolute, and also of the out-breath, through which the Real comes into existence. In that moment-by-moment blossoming of the emptiness lie all the potential and possibilities of life. Here is the blank page waiting for the brush stroke, waiting for life to recreate itself anew. And we are part of this moment-by-moment creation, the formless opening into form. We are co-creators in life's manifestation of love.

5

TWO POLES OF LOVE

—⎯⎯⎯

Lord of the Universe,
Prabhu Sovereign Spirit
Beneficent and Merciful Allah
My Infinite One,
At Thy Command only
Will I carry out the Pilgrimage of Life
For the Love of All Created by Thee
And for Thy glory.

Prayer

Life spins on a single axis of love with two poles—love for the Creator and love for the creation.

These are the poles of remembrance; we remember the Absolute beyond all that is or will be, and we remember the Absolute manifest throughout the created world—the smallest cricket, the wildest ocean, the most beautiful sunset. This is the primal duality of the Absolute—Creator and creation, transcendent and immanent, masculine and feminine.

This essential duality is described in many spiritual traditions. In Chinese philosophy it shows up as the forces of *yang* and *yin*, the masculine and feminine principles. In Hinduism it is imaged as *Shiva*, the abiding principle, and

Shakti, the life force within creation, and also as *Purusha* and *Prakriti*, spirit and matter. In Buddhism, reality is described as both emptiness and also compassion, imaged by the living Buddhas and Bodhisattvas born from the emptiness.[1] In the mystical arm of Judaism, the *shekhinah* is the indwelling aspect of God, in contrast to the transcendent God.

For Sufis, these dual aspects are reflected in the Names of God, the Names of Majesty and of Beauty—*jalāl* and *jamāl*—which the mystic experiences as awe and intimacy. Bowed down before the transcendent, all-powerful God, we are in awe. Opening to a love that is closer to us than our jugular vein, we know the greatest intimacy possible.

Neither of these aspects of the Absolute is more real than the other. The primal two is not other than the One.

In the West we have inherited a spiritual culture that has distorted both aspects of the Real. We have reduced the true majesty of the Absolute to an image of God as a distant father figure whom we expect to either judge or take care of us, his children. We see in creation not the awe-inspiring beauty of the Absolute revealing itself in form, but rather a resource there for our own gratification. Instead of following our longing for the tremendous love and intimacy of the Real, we often identify this longing as depression or settle for secondhand relationships focused on our ego's needs and desires.

These distorted images work together to distance us from the Real. The concept of a distant father God has diverted our attention from life, divorcing us from the experience of ourselves as part of a divine creation, of its mystery and wonder, the experience of the sacredness of our own bodies and the Earth itself. And all the ways we mistake self-gratification and romantic ideals for love veil us from our innermost desire for real intimacy with the Divine, and from the aspect of ourselves that will give anything for this love affair that is absolutely—and sometimes violently—uncompromising.

Without knowing the awe of real power, and without knowing the intimacy of embodied and transformative love, we have become lost in a world of shadows, and life itself has darkened.

MAJESTY AND BEAUTY

The power of the Creator is the power of "I am that I am,"[2] the power of "That which is." This indefinable and unreachable aspect of Reality is described by Ibn 'Arabī:

> He is and there is with Him no before or after, nor above nor below, nor far nor near, nor union nor division, nor how nor where nor place. He is now as He was, He is the One without oneness and the Single without singleness. He is the very existence of the Outward and the very existence of the Inward.[3]

The incomparable nature of the Absolute is unreachable—"beyond even our idea of the beyond." In Sufism, it has been said that one should never even contemplate the Absolute because one cannot ever know or reach it. A *hadīth* states, "Think about the creation but do not think about the Creator."[4] One can contemplate the qualities of the Absolute—the Divine Names and Attributes—but not That. As the Sufi mystic Sanā'ī imagines God saying,

> Whatever comes to your mind that I am that—
>   I am not that!
> Whatever has room in your understanding
>   that I would be like this—I am not like this![5]

This is similar to the ancient Hindu practice of *neti neti*, acknowledging, "not this, not this," as one travels the path to the Real.

The mystic remembers this majestic aspect of the Absolute, the essential *fact* of the Absolute. It is other. It is indefinable. It is unreachable. "No one knows God but God."

In Sufism we bow down before our unknowable Beloved. We are at the feet of That. We are the servants of a Master that cannot be named. Mystics live this truth in a state of complete unknowing because we cannot know That to which we belong. We remain in a constant state of prayer before the majesty of God, a state of total submission.

Living this primal axis of remembrance, mystics avoid the unnecessary power dynamics that entrap most people. In relation to such power, what power dynamics can we play? The servant is focused on the One that cannot be known or named and is always revealing Itself anew. We spin on an axis aligned with the Real, spinning faster than the dynamics of those around us. We are essentially free, in a state of attention and submission.

It is important to acknowledge that there is a violent side of divine Majesty, which has been described as the "wrath of God." In contemporary spiritual culture we rarely acknowledge this dimension. But historically there are many stories of God's violence. The biblical flood is such an expression:

> And behold, I, even I, do bring a flood of waters upon the earth, to destroy all flesh, wherein is the breath of life, from under heaven; and every thing that is in the earth shall die.[6]

And in the words of Christ, "Think not that I am come to send peace on earth: I came not to send peace, but a sword."[7]

Many great saints have submitted to this aspect of God, including St. Teresa of Avila, who was driven by inspiration and divine guidance to establish numerous convents in her new Carmelite order. During one treacherous journey to a distant destination, she is said to have been thrown from her horse while crossing a river. She yelled out to God: *"Dear Lord, if this is how You treat Your friends, it is no wonder You have so few!"*

She veils with humor both the great challenges of service to God, of surrendering again and again to a God that violently demands absolute obedience, and the fact that few are capable of such a relationship.

In Sufism, this aspect of God is known as "the sword of La *ilāha*"—the sword that cuts through the illusions of life, affirming only that *There is no god but God!*

In the West—and in America particularly in reaction to its Puritan, God-fearing heritage—there is tremendous fear of real authority, and a deep need for a comforting and reassuring God. But this aspect of the Absolute is not reassuring. It does not treat everyone equally; it is not gentle. In fact, it can destroy you, your ego, your sense of self, your patterns of control, everything that separates you from the One you love. In Rūmī's words, we are "the friends of the One who slaughters His friends."[8] This love destroys what needs to be destroyed.

A relationship with this aspect of the Absolute is not safe. It is not contained; it cannot be controlled. It is alive, it is present, and it has tremendous power. It is real and it demands that you be real and make a commitment to that inside you which is real.

In fact, if a seeker cannot use the sword that affirms *There is no god but God*—if she cannot wield the power that has no power dynamics, the sword that cuts away any illusion or false sense of self and confirms in an instant that which is real in herself—then there comes a time when the spiritual path closes to her, when she can go no further.

This aspect of the Real must be acknowledged for what it is. Otherwise the seeker goes round and round at the same level, spinning at the same vibration, incapable of leaving behind what is no longer true—caught in the same level of illusion, in the patterns of the ego, or the dynamics of a spiritualized sense of self.

For many, the other aspect of the Absolute in the primal duality of the Real is easier to relate to. This is the tremendous intimacy and love contained in the Sufi Name *jamāl*, the beauty of God, a beauty and tenderness alive in the heart and in the core of life itself. In the intimacy of this beauty you experience your Beloved as "nearer to you than yourself to yourself." Here you find the sweetness and ecstasy known only to lovers.

Religious and spiritual traditions throughout time have emphasized this aspect of the Divine. As St. John

70

declared in his epistle, "Whoever does not love does not know God, for God is love."[9]

The divine aspect of Beauty, like Majesty, is free of all power dynamics because it is complete. As Rūmī described it, "Subtle degrees of domination and servitude are what you know as love. But love is different, it arrives complete—just there like the moon at the window."[10]

Most of us are caught in the ego's dynamics of domination and servitude, patterns of control and dependence, security and insecurity. We search for psychological safety in one or the other of these opposites, and we have projected these dynamics into an image of love and also spiritual life. But as Rūmī says, divine love is very different—it is complete. It is free. Within this love we are ourselves, alone with the Beloved.

Many of those drawn to spiritual paths are called by this love. We thirst for it. We long to be drawn into this oneness, this intimacy, this ecstatic intoxication:

> There is some kiss we want
> with our whole lives,
> the touch of Spirit on the body.
>
> Seawater begs the pearl
> to break its shell …[11]

But like the Majesty of God, this aspect as well has been misunderstood. This is not a love that always makes you feel good. It is not the love of romance novels or the love of greeting cards. It is the love of the Absolute. It seeps through all defenses, permeates a human being from the inside out, disintegrates what is not real and takes a seeker into a boundaryless union that is too alive, too demanding, too complete ever to be secure.

This love "breaks the shell of the pearl" and unveils the soul.

This same love also permeates all of creation. Indigenous peoples have always acknowledged it within the Earth and all creatures, a love that connects us all together. Tatanka Yotanka (Sitting Bull) expresses this:

Behold, my brothers, the spring has come;
The earth has received the embraces of the sun and
We shall soon see the results of that love!
Every seed is awakened and so has all animal life.
It is through this mysterious power that we too
Have our being and therefore yield to our neighbors,
Even our animal neighbors, the same right as
Ourselves to inhabit this land.

The axis of love invites us from the confines of the ego into the vastness of a love that spins every atom. It has never been easy to accept the invitation. Ikkyu, the 15th-century Zen poet, chided the priests of his own time:

Every day, priests minutely examine the Law
And endlessly chant complicated sutras.
Before doing that, though, they should learn
How to read the love letters sent by the wind
And rain, the snow and moon.

The intimacy and tenderness of the Absolute reveals Itself where It wants. In one moment it is the salt smell of the sea, the sunlight in a field, the clear chill of autumn, the

72

dewdrops on a spider's web. Another moment it is in the heart, an unbelievable sweetness, the total belonging to an unnameable presence. Along the axis of love, we know real belonging. It works with the majesty of God to draw us nearer and nearer, ultimately in devotion and complete surrender, until we realize that we are the oneness that includes all of creation, we are the love alive in every cell.

THE RELATIONSHIP TO A TEACHER

Most individuals cannot relate directly to the Absolute, whether through the intimate or the awe-inspiring aspect, so for many the relationship starts with a teacher. When a teacher is connected to a living tradition both these aspects of the Absolute can be transmitted to the student. The teacher is an intermediary—a stepping stone—for a relationship that is ultimately only between lover and Beloved.

This relationship requires that the teacher be in total submission. Otherwise, power dynamics will corrupt the process, block the transmission. We have seen these power dynamics play out through history as well as in contemporary spirituality, from Catholic Church abuses to Buddhist teachers having inappropriate relationships with their students.

There is no safeguard against such dynamics except finding a teacher who is absolutely submitted to God, who has been made empty. Then the relationship is founded on one need only—the need of the Real.

When a seeker meets her teacher, she can be given a quality of love she's never had before. One is loved so completely, accepted unconditionally. This is a relationship of soul-to-soul, heart-to-heart. Through the relationship with the teacher, the soul, which is made of love, is awakened and infused with even more love, and it flows throughout the whole human being. It flows from the soul into the emotional body, into the etheric body, even into the physical body. There can be experiences of great tenderness, a sense of nearness, love, and longing. The seeker can merge into that love.

This love is not separate from power. The majesty aspect and the beauty aspect are one, spiraling together in service to Truth. There are numerous stories of this degree of devotion and submission, love and fear, intimacy and awe, including great saints of all traditions. Buddhism has historically emphasized the role of the teacher and the transmission from teacher to disciple. The Tibetan saint Milarepa who submitted to the will of his teacher, Marpa, is one example.

Milarepa was trained very simply in a way of total submission. When he met his teacher, Marpa, he was not given spiritual practices. Instead, Marpa directed Milarepa to build him a house, which he did. But Marpa was not pleased and told his disciple to take it down and build it in a different location. Which Milarepa did. This took months of labor. And even so, Marpa was not pleased and told Milarepa to move the structure again. Which he did, of course, because he understood the thread of power and devotion that linked these two human beings together through many lifetimes. This went on for quite some time. In Milarepa's songs, he says:

> After a hard journey I arrived there.
> For six years and eight months I stayed there

With him, my gracious Father Guru, Marpa.
For him I built many houses,
One with courtyards and nine storeys;
Only after this did he accept me.[12]

At the beginning, Milarepa resisted taking down and
rebuilding the houses again and again. It seemed senseless,
without purpose. But finally he surrendered; he unconditionally accepted the will of his teacher. And soon after
he was accepted by his teacher, he was told to leave. The
training in submission was complete. Having surrendered
his personal will, his higher will could incarnate through
him. He left his teacher and went out into the world, com-
mitting himself to the pursuit of Truth.

Many don't understand the difference between personal will and higher will. The higher will belongs to the
Self, to our higher destiny and the will of God. It requires
great discrimination to identify and align with the higher
will rather than the will of the ego. But through the grace of
the tradition and the relationship with the teacher, the ego
learns to bow down and so the higher will is incarnated.
When this happens, the soul is what guides the human
being, and the awakened soul is always in submission to
Truth. And the soul belongs to love.

The Sufi teacher Irina Tweedie had great love for her
sheikh. In her book, *Daughter of Fire*, she describes feeling
an intimacy that was unlike anything she had ever experienced. Her heart would be resting in his heart in infinite
peace, despite the commotion around her, the people
coming to talk to him, and the activities of the household.

At the same time she sensed his remoteness, his for-
bidding look, a hard, cold, stony face. And he often treated

her with seeming cruelty, psychologically torturing her, ignoring her, leaving her feeling desolate and abandoned.

Years later she said that people would ask about her spiritual training, "Would you do it again?" She replied first that she could not; she was too old and her body could not bear it—the heat, the pain, the heartache. But then she said she would not need to because she would just say "yes" at the very beginning.

Through this intertwining of Majesty and Beauty, power and love, her teacher taught her to surrender, to become dust at his feet. Only when that happens can one unconditionally follow the will of the teacher. And often only after the training is finished does one realize the real love of the teacher for the disciple that was there from the very beginning—the closed circle of love.

Real submission may begin as an inner battle, but finally it is a state of grace in which something within the seeker bows down, first before that within the teacher that is the will of God, and then before God alone. That is the traditional training. And it includes a willingness to be with both aspects of the Absolute—the violence and severity of *jalāl* and the great love and mercy of *jamāl*.

This relationship belongs to the deep secret that the whole of creation is in submission before its Creator. Everything bows down before God, every atom praises its Lord.

In this relationship, the mystic has *no* power. It is that complete submission that enables the energy of the Absolute to come through, into this plane of reality. The individual must be in a state of submission, or the energy of the Absolute hits the ego, creating inflation, or it terrifies or damages the individual. If this happens, the mystic simply cannot function, and God needs us to function as the human beings we are. The Beloved needs us as lovers:

> Verily, I have servants among My servants who
> love Me, and I love them, and they long for Me, and
> I long for them and they look at Me, and I look at
> them … and I see what they bear for My sake and
> I hear what they complain from My love.[13]

Through this bond of love, born of intimacy and awe, the lover connects the worlds together, the formless inner world and the outer world of life's beauty and form.

THE SUBSTANCE OF THE SOUL

There is a substance in the soul of a mystic that knows the two as One, that can offer creation back to the Creator in an act of remembrance. It is through this remembering that we bring the truth of what is real into this world of illusion and in doing so, redeem this world, nurture it, and reveal its essential unity.

This world is starving. Through our collective attitude we are isolating the outer world from its spiritual core. Our focus on materialism, our denial of the sacred within creation, has alienated us from the source of life. The river of life no longer runs pure—its water is polluted outwardly and inwardly. The symbolic worlds that traditionally connected the outer life with the meaning and sacred nourishment that come from within have been desecrated. The separation from the sacred and the Source is denying life an essential ingredient, a quality of spirit.

The work of the mystic today is to reconnect life with the Source. There are individuals who have been born to do this work, to reconnect the world with what is real, to align the world with the poles of love. If one has come into this world to be of service in this way, the substance of the soul has a special light. There is a different vibration in such a human being, because this substance carries a very particular imprint. It belongs to both the Creator and the creation, and is in itself a link of love between the worlds.

This substance is the most precious thing in one's life. It is like liquid gold. It is part of the core of our being and it connects us to a certain fabric of life. From a spiritual perspective, it is really why we are here. It is the deepest purpose of our incarnation—the very meaning of life.

At the beginning of our life, the substance is dormant; it is like a seed. It is just a possibility that has yet to wake up. It's not yet fully alive. But through the right attitude, through the willingness to serve, and through grace, the substance starts to move, to come alive. The seeker comes to know this substance as the real pilgrim on the path, the real offering of the heart. And then she begins to live this imprint of love, this offering to life and the Beloved. This is when the heart becomes truly alive.

From that time on, the path cannot go back. It has its own momentum; it takes you where it wants to go. You are the vehicle for the divine substance within the heart. This is the esoteric meaning of being a real human being: *Man is My secret and I am his secret. And that is the Secret of secrets.*

When this substance is awake, it is always in conversation. And you learn to listen. It whispers to you secrets about yourself, about love, about the heart, about life. And it whispers from your heart into life, it breathes back into life what we are given as lovers of Truth. Life becomes a companion, a friend, and you learn how to come alive with love. A beautiful and magical interface takes place between all that had seemed separate but is now in constant communion.

If the mystic lives her light, if she remembers what is Real in herself and in life, this substance of the soul permeates the cells of her body—every cell rotates around the axis of love with joy and remembrance. And this body alive with remembrance is not separate from the body of life, the Earth, just as the individual soul is not separate from the world soul. The substance, the light, moves through all levels of reality; it flows through the worlds.

Everything in the life of the mystic becomes a pulsating remembrance that nourishes the whole.

Life needs the substance alive in a human being who has surrendered, who is willing to be of service. Such a human being is a living organism of light and love amidst all the dense thought-forms of this world, amidst all the desires of material or spiritual acquisition and life's many demands.

In our spiritual culture with its materialistic orientation, we have forgotten how mystics carry part of the divine consciousness of life. Mystics carry the brain cells of divine remembrance that belong to life. Without that essential ingredient, life cannot redeem itself, just as we cannot be redeemed without the grace of the Absolute: grace as a living substance that comes into life—that is part of life—that awakens life to what it really is through our hearts. It is time for mystics to remember this truth of union, that we are part of life's divine secret with a role to play in the expression of God through the myriad forms of life.

This divine substance has a deep rhythm. It is as though, for that substance, the whole of the lifetime is the breath. For that spark within the soul, all the infinite moments of one's lifetime are present in the in-breath and out-breath. The out-breath is the journey into the world. And the in-breath is the return journey. And those two become the one: the one breath. Our whole life's journey is unified in our knowing that we live only for the sake of the Real: "For the Love of All Created by Thee and for Thy glory."

Bound together in love, the inner and outer worlds can start to sing. And it is just one breath. One's life—one's whole life, everything that we thought was important and everything that was unimportant and was irrelevant—all of it, if it is breathed correctly, is one breath.

It is the breath of God.

It is the song of Truth.

6

THE MAGIC OF CREATION

—⟨⟨⟨⟨⟨⟩⟩⟩⟩⟩—

The world is charged with the grandeur of God.
It will flame out like shining from shook foil.
Gerard Manley Hopkins[1]

The Creator is alive within creation. The Absolute lives in every atom, every cell.

Just as human beings contain a sacred substance within our soul, there is a substance in the core of life that is real. It is like a seed of Truth, a spark of the light of the Absolute.

This substance of creation can be interacted with. Human beings can engage in a unique dialogue between the substance in our souls and the substance in creation— a dialogue of light upon light. Through this dialogue, the kaleidoscope of life reveals the one essence of the Absolute, and the Absolute celebrates Itself.

This is not the same dialogue as the soul's light interacting with the light of the inner planes, a disembodied divinity, which is how most of us understand spirituality. It is the light of the soul interacting with the light hidden within the material dimension—with God incarnate. Through this dialogue we come to know the Divine in the world around us. In Sufism, these different forms of witnessing are acknowledged:

There are two kinds of witnessing: One is to behold the singularity of the Sacred Essence, stripped from the veil of external manifestations. The other is to contemplate within the curtain of manifestations. This is what the Sūfīs call "the vision of Oneness in multiplicity."[2]

Through this dialogue the Creator uses the mirror of humanity to reveal Itself to Itself, as expressed in the *hadīth qudsī, "I was a hidden treasure and I wanted to be known, so I created the world."*

The more awake the human consciousness, the clearer is the real nature of creation. As the "eye of the heart" opens, the practices of the path enable the clarity of real perception, the perception of the soul, through which the mystic no longer sees "through a glass darkly." She becomes the eyes of God in this world.

Historically we have forgotten this aspect—this feminine, embodied side of God. And we have forgotten the language of how our souls speak to what is real within life, this conversation with creation. Instead, we are entrapped in our individual and collective ego, seeing life only through a consciousness clouded by our desires and our fears, reducing the dynamic divinity of life to "a collection of objects."[3]

But this hidden mystical substance in creation is waiting to be interacted with, and it holds the essence of the work of co-creation, through which humanity can creatively participate in the moment-by-moment revelation of the Divine within the world, the moment-by-moment re-creation of the world.

In the past, various traditions have guided this type of work. In the West, the alchemists held the secret of the light hidden within matter, working symbolically to transmute lead into gold. In their retorts and crucibles they were working not just with chemicals and minerals but with the spiritual energies within matter. Carl Jung talked about uncovering the mystery of the *lumen dei* and the *lumen naturae*. He identified the *lumen dei* as the disembodied light of the Divine, which we normally associate with a transcendent God. And he described the *lumen naturae* as the hidden light within creation, referring to it as "the universal and scintillating fire in the light of nature which carries the heavenly spirit within it."[4]

The practice of alchemy rested on the understanding that "as above, so below." The light in creation is the manifestation of the one light, as expressed in the core alchemical text, Hermes' *Emerald Tablet*:

The father of all perfection in the whole world
    is here.
Its force of power is entire if it be converted
    into earth.

The "conversion to earth" is the great work of the human being to know, reveal, and honor the Creator in creation, thereby releasing the "force of power" that belongs to the Absolute.

A similar tradition belongs to Sufism. The early Sufi Dhū'l-Nūn was "famous for his involvement with alchemy,"[5] and there is a whole hidden alchemical tradition within Sufism that honors this transformative element within creation. This is reflected in the mystical importance of the secret of the word *"Kun!"* ["Be!"], which expresses the mystery of the creative aspect of God that brings life into being. It has been said that between the *K* and the *N* of *"Kun,"* there is an entire universe.

And of course shamanistic traditions have always honored the spiritual energies embodied in the plants and animals of Earth. All healing traditions have honored the incarnated light.

The relationship of the light of human consciousness with the light within creation—the human soul with the soul of the world—is at the foundation of our collective evolution. This mystery used to be understood in our collective consciousness; our daily lives were a reflection of this dialogue. In the past, when women ground corn as they chanted sacred songs, they were developing and honoring a profound relationship of inner and outer, of women and corn and the whole mystery of fertility. The earth that is planted with the sacred seed, the man who harvests the corn with reverence, the woman who grinds the corn, the family or tribe sustained by corn, the corn who is known as a goddess—all are nourished within a sacred communion.

The Christian rite of communion, with its emphasis on the bread and the wine as the real flesh and blood of Christ, retains a hint of this recognition of the spiritual reality within the material world. The physical bread contains a spiritual bread; the wine contains a spiritual wine.

For many centuries we shared our evolution with the Earth and all that belongs to the Earth; both our evolution and the Earth's depended upon that connection. But today this is lost. The understanding of the magic of creation that belonged to those eras is forgotten. In today's materialistic society we have separated ourselves so far from the Earth and the simple realities of life, controlled so many of the ways we interact with nature, turned our religions so completely toward the image of a transcendent God, that this relationship to the spiritual mysteries of Earth has been severed.[6]

What we don't understand is that this separation means that the whole of life cannot evolve. Nor can humanity, as separate from that whole, evolve. We can only evolve as One—as a single, living whole.

The next step in our collective evolution is to recognize the divinity of life with a consciousness that sees and knows the One at the heart of the many, to reclaim an ancient knowing of life's sacredness.

THE SACRED NAMES OF CREATION

There was a time, long ago, when the lords of light—the masters of the inner planes—worked together with humanity to awaken the world. This was the time of naming, when all of the multiplicity of creation was named for the first time. Through the power of its names, creation came alive to its higher purpose. Each thing that was named, each flower and tree, each animal and insect, became conscious of its true nature and purpose in the web of creation. This knowing, quite different from conscious knowing as we understand it today, is rather an instinctual, innate knowing belonging more to the spirit of each life-form. Through it, the world came alive with the magic of naming.

The sacred names of creation were also used to make a relationship between humanity and the created world. Every plant, every animal on Earth had a name, and humanity knew these names. The names of animals evoked their power, the names of plants revealed their healing properties, the names of rivers and mountains ensured that the world was kept in harmony and balance. Humanity's knowing of the power and purpose of Earth awakened Earth to its own power, its magic and sacred meaning.

Knowing the real names of creation has tremendous impact, in the same way that recognizing an individual for who she really is can change her life. Something deep and real is confirmed and energized. Many indigenous traditions still carry an understanding of the names of creation, even if the names themselves have been lost. Australian Aboriginal traditions recognize the "dreamtime" beyond past, present, and future, in which ancestral beings wandered over the land singing out the name of everything that crossed their path—animals, plants, rocks, water holes—and so sang the world into existence.

In this time before the beginning, before the great Fall when the Earth was still pristine, humanity engaged with the power of the names and created a new relationship between the Creator and the created world. There was a purity of intention in this relationship between humanity and the Earth and all its myriad creatures; it honored the sacred energies of life. The partnership had a divine meaning—it helped awaken the light hidden within the physical world, which could then fulfill its highest purpose of reflecting the Absolute back to Itself. And through it, magic was awakened within the created world, and the seeds of consciousness were sown.

From this communion between humanity and creation were born the daily rituals that honored all of life, the rituals of planting and harvesting, the rites of hearth and home, death and birth, chanting, singing and dance— all providing ways to honor the energies within creation, ways for the light of the soul of humanity to interact with the soul of the world.

The soul of humanity and the soul of the world were bonded together, and the Earth showed her generosity. It was a communion, now only remembered in myth and scripture as the time when God walked in the Garden of Eden before Adam and Eve hid themselves from Him, before they knew they were naked, before they were ashamed.

This was the time when, as told in the Bible, Adam— the archetypal first man—gave creation its names, forming this sacred bond (Genesis 2:19–20). In the Qur'an it is told as when "God taught Adam the names" (2:31).

This was the beginning of the covenant between humanity and creation.

So much was given at this time. The Creator had so many ways to love creation, to give to creation. The human heart and consciousness were a vehicle for this abundance, and in turn, the heart of the Earth reciprocated.

In this primordial time, the power of the Word, the *logos* principle, and the names of creation brought light and consciousness into creation. It was the awakening of the Earth, when after millions of years of unconsciousness, the world began to know its purpose as an expression of God, and each created thing began to awaken to its unique expression of sacredness:

As kingfishers catch fire, dragonflies dráw fláme;
As tumbled over rim in roundy wells
Stones ring; like each tucked string tells,
    each hung bell's
  Bow swung finds tongue tó fling out
    broad its name;
Each mortal thing does one thing and the same:
Deals out that being indoors each one dwells;
Selves—goes itself; myself it speaks and spells,
Crying Whát I do is me: for that I came.[7]

The world known as it is, is quite different from the world created by our desires and projections, by the endless patterns of our mind and the recycling of our memories that we call existence. Those who for an instant have awakened, had a glimpse of what the Zen masters call *satori*, know this simple experience of truth—when the butterfly is glimpsed as a butterfly, when the sweetness of plum is truly tasted. It is a reality without comparison or contradiction that communicates its true nature to us directly rather than as interpreted through our mind or psyche. In such moments we are really alive, awake rather than dreaming.

The mystery and power of the names of creation remains; the primal magic woven between the world of light and the world of creation still lives. The Earth is calling for us to awaken and remember this primal bond with her. This bond was never severed, despite the many ways we have tried to destroy it, despite all the stories of separation we tell ourselves. But it has weakened, like a gossamer thread buffeted by a terrible storm. It is time to remember this bond, to honor this relationship, to know that it is the only true foundation of our shared future.

THE POWER WITHIN MATTER

The light within the Earth, what the alchemists called the *lumen naturae*, is a primal source of energy and power that has yet to be fully accessed by humanity. It belongs to our natural relationship to life, to creation and its sacred nature. This energy source can once again become accessible as humanity remembers its place in the whole and relates to all life with an understanding of oneness—of unity and multi-dimensional interdependence. We cannot work with Earth's light, nor will we know the real names of creation, through a consciousness of separation or duality. We need to claim the consciousness of oneness that is waiting for us.

As we awaken to this sacred unity at the core of the world, life itself awakens, because we are not separate from the whole. This power within life gradually becomes available, and we can learn how to use it. It belongs to the magical nature of life, life's ability to change and evolve. It carries the ancient wisdom of the archetypal world, an understanding of the energy patterns within life, the grids of power within the Earth. Working with this power within creation, we can reclaim our heritage as guardians of the Earth, of its sacred and mysterious ways. We can once again be initiated into the deeper levels of existence, the now-hidden ways that energy flows within and around the world.

The patterns of power within the Earth are an ancient secret, part of the knowledge we have lost over the centuries.[8] As we have blinkered our consciousness into seeing only the outer appearances of the material world, we have lost our understanding of its inner, hidden dimensions. Our ideas, beliefs, and attitudes have silenced the song of the Earth and closed the door on her light.

In our current collective unconsciousness we carry a strong sense of being at war with matter, of needing to overcome or conquer all that is of the Earth. We are trapped by ideas about the constrictions of matter, and still fight against its apparent limitations. Our attitudes and our actions are killing life; our stories tell us we are separate from the Source. And so we are caught in a cycle of self-destruction.

The physical world needs to be re-aligned with its own energy source, with the life force within it. The quickest way to align anything or anybody is by recognizing its true nature. Through humanity's recognition of the sacredness of life—the divinity of everything on Earth—and through our reverence, the consciousness of our light can interact with the light in matter. The highest principle can come alive again within creation and release the energy waiting there.

This energy that comes from the very core of creation can heal the Earth and the psyche of humanity. It will reveal the unity and "interbeing" of all of creation, as expressed in the numinous image of *Indra's Net* from the Mahayana Buddhist tradition:

> Here the universe is seen as an infinite net; wherever the threads cross there is a clear shining pearl that reflects and is itself reflected in every other pearl. Each pearl is an individual consciousness—whether of a human being, an animal, a plant, a cell or an atom—so a change in one pearl, however small, makes a change in all the other pearls, each one both singular and responsive to the whole.[9]

As matter becomes aligned with its true nature, it begins to vibrate at a higher frequency. It begins to sing. This song is one of the ways it will heal itself. Song has always been a magical way of healing, and the song of the world has tremendous power. In it, all the names of creation are remembered and awakened and celebrated. This song knows the name of God and sings of God in every leaf and every lake and every human being.

The song of the world belongs to the primary nature of all that is. It is life's sacredness expressing itself, remembering its Source. But we need to listen for it; we need to hear it. We need to celebrate the song. Our ancestors' knowing that everything they could see was sacred was not something taught but something deeply, instinctively heard.

The "sacred" is not something primarily religious or even spiritual. It is not a quality we need to learn or to develop. We all have within us a sense of the sacred, a sense of reverence, however we may articulate it. It is as natural as sunlight, as necessary as breathing. It belongs to our connection with the original Adam.

We each carry this primal knowing within our consciousness, even if we have forgotten it. It is a fundamental recognition of the wonder, beauty, and divine nature of the world. When we sense that our world is not just a physical, mechanistic, or chance-driven reality but that there is a deeper mystery within and around it, we are sensing the sacred nature of creation; we are hearing its primal song. If we remember the sacred we will find ourselves in a world as whole as it is holy. However we may call this mystery, it permeates all of creation. It may be more easily felt in certain places—in ancient groves, beneath star-filled skies, in temples or cathedrals, in the chords of music. But this is a mystery that belongs to all that exists—there is nothing that is separate from it. As such it celebrates the unity that is within and around us, the oneness of which we are a part. Our sense of the sacred is a recognition that we are a part of this deeper all-embracing mystery.

Once we allow our consciousness to touch into this greater mystery, we will find that life will speak to us as it spoke to our ancestors. It will remind us of how to live in harmony with creation and how to restore the balance that is intrinsic to life. And it will give us the energy, the power, and the knowledge needed to heal and redeem our wounded world. It will help us to break free from the nightmare of materialism that is strangling us, so that together with the Earth we can give birth to a story of real global transformation.

INSTANT BY INSTANT

The transformation of the world is a science. Just as the spiritual transformation of a human being needs to follow a precise and careful course, so does this global evolution have specific guidelines. For example, there are specific ways to work with the energy within creation, just as there is a science in the reflection of light from the inner to the outer. This knowledge is part of our heritage even as it is at times hidden from us. As Ibn 'Arabī describes this mystery,

> God deposited within man knowledge of all things, then prevented him from perceiving

what He had deposited.... No one knows what is within himself until it is unveiled to him instant by instant.[10]

A dynamic blueprint of how life truly is—how the inner worlds relate to the outer and how the human being mediates between dimensions—exists within us. This blueprint accords with specific laws, known by many indigenous traditions as "the original instructions." These laws are the spiritual guiding principles of humanity and all life-forms on the planet. They are part of the cellular structure of creation, part of its DNA.

The work of the mystic is to be part of this transformation, to add the ingredient of spiritual consciousness as life starts to know itself and sing its sacred song. This note of divine consciousness is a catalyst to the next cycle of revelation. Our journey is not to return to the indigenous consciousness of our ancestors, or to a purely transcendent consciousness, but *to combine the two, above and below.* We need to reclaim an understanding of the spiritual dimension of creation, of its living oneness, from the perspective of the individualized consciousness that we have claimed over the last era. Consciousness is the most vital ingredient in the process of transformation, and it is the combination of the light of individual consciousness and the light within the Earth that will help awaken the world and humanity to our next cycle of shared evolution.

But it will not be easy. Collectively humanity has put up tremendous barriers to the conscious awareness of life's sacredness. We have allowed attitudes of separation and isolation, together with a concept of matter as "dead," to keep us from real awareness of life's depths where oneness waits to work its magic, where the archetypal energies are waiting for our conscious participation.

Spiritual seekers, sadly, have often woven into these collective attitudes the energy of an aspiration that focuses on their own individual well-being, their own "awakening," forgetting or dismissing the larger dimension of the whole. Some seekers have traditionally turned away from life, while others have become, in recent years, caught in the illusions of self-development. For many seekers it will feel that there is much to lose by giving our longing to life, by recognizing that only as a part of a living whole is there any real purpose to transformation. They have forgotten the wonder of the moment in the garden, the spider's web caught in a ray of sunshine, dew sparkling with light.

Many of us will need to work hard to let go of past attitudes and attune our attention to the instant-by-instant revelations of divine beauty and presence. So much has to be given up in order to return to a purity of intention, to that moment when life is simple and sacred.

But as we become more and more aware of divine presence, our consciousness will reconnect to the primal structure of life instinctually known to our ancestors.[11] As this connection is established, we enter the depths of the Earth and work with the energies there. "*Visita interiora terrae*," said the alchemists: "Visit the interior of the Earth."

The mysteries of the future reside throughout this reconnection with the living Earth, which will enable spirit and matter to combine in a new way. Then we will know above and below as one and reawaken to the magic and wonder within life. We all have access to the knowledge of Adam, the first man, the knowledge of the names of creation, which belong to the divine "secrets of heaven and earth" (Qur'an 3:33). And this reawakening will give us new understanding of these secrets, constellating a new cycle of divine revelation.

Knowing the true purpose of the created world is part of our divine heritage; it is the thread from the past that is needed to create the tapestry of the future. But this work of co-creation will not be easy. There are forces working against it—patterns of darkness we have unknowingly created. This darkness is slowly covering the world, cutting us off from the Source and the energies within creation, as well as the light of our own higher consciousness. It is denying us the possibility of real transformation, of writing the next chapter of the story of the world, of the revelation of the Absolute. If we are to work with the light of the Divine we also need to recognize and respect the veils of darkness.

7

VEILS OF LIGHT, VEILS OF DARKNESS

━━◅▰▱▰▱▰▰▱▰▱▸━━

Darkness is your candle.

Rūmī

Working with the light within creation, the *lumen naturae*, is perhaps one of the most important spiritual tasks of the moment. But developing this relationship of light to light, of soul to world soul, requires more than the simple intent to walk in a sacred manner or to honor moments of communion with nature. These are important elements, but there is more that needs to be understood and experienced.

Particularly, we need to understand how our relationship to the light within creation affects and is affected by the illusions of the world, the veils that separate us from a direct experience of life. These veils exist. Some veils are part of the natural order of creation and ultimately serve to reveal the Absolute. But other veils distort the Absolute and are designed to keep humanity from experiencing anything real, to keep us distracted. Many of these veils have been created in recent years and are covering the world in darkness.

Too many of us are naïve about the spiritual path, unaware of the extent of the darkness that hides the Truth.

But it serves nothing to remain blind to the spiritual realities of our current time. We need to acknowledge that creation needs our spiritual as well as physical attention—that we need to care for the soul of the world as well as its soil. And we need to be aware of what obstructs this relationship.

Many spiritual traditions acknowledge the existence of veils that hide the light of Truth and hide our own divine nature from us. These veils belong to the dance of life—the hide-and-seek of the Beloved within creation. We are caught, trapped in the illusions of life by our desires as well as our ego's identity and sense of a separate self. Much of the traditional work of any spiritual path is to renounce our desires, dissolve or burn down the ego's experience of illusion and separation, and find the thread of Truth within our heart and within life. Each path has its own methods of seeing past the dream of life's appearances. As the Buddha directed through the Diamond Sutra:

> So I tell you—Thus shall you think of all
> this fleeting world:
> A star at dawn, a bubble floating in a stream;
> A flash of lightning in a summer cloud,
> A flickering lamp, a phantom, or a dream.

Until the veils are lifted, there is no knowing what is real within this "fleeting world." There is little real in our experience of life.

But the seeker cannot bypass the veils that separate her from the Truth. These veils both distract and protect. If they did not exist, the seeker would be burned away immediately by the light of the Absolute:

God has seventy-thousand veils of light and seventy-thousand veils of darkness. Were they to be removed, the glories of His Face would burn away everything perceived by the sight of His creatures.[1]

Traditionally, the seeker engages with the veils and gradually moves through them. This process has been well documented. The stages of the path might be imaged by the ox-herding pictures in Zen, the stages of prayer as delineated by St. Teresa of Avila, or the seven valleys of the soul's journey in 'Attār's Sufi parable of the quest, *The Conference of the Birds*. Each stage is a part of an unfolding revelation that takes one closer and closer to the Truth.

The veils of illusion might be seductive and they might be terrifying, but their essential nature is to point to Truth beyond appearance. For example, Rūmī writes that "a woman is God shining through subtle veils."[2] And Jāmī tells the story of Zulaikha, who falls in love with the image of the divine lover in the form of Yūsuf. Initially, captivated by his incomparable form, she is "oblivious to the underlying reality." The real beauty is "hidden behind the veil of mystery," and her journey is to find the source of this beauty, rather than its reflection in the dance of forms. Jāmī advises, "Now that you have seen the reflection, make haste for the source ... The reflection is as ephemeral as a rose's blush: if you want permanence, turn towards the source."[3]

These veils are part of God's great play. As Ibn 'Arabī says, "We are veiled from Thee only through Thee."

But the veils within creation also have a magical numinosity that is there to seduce us, to "lead us into temptation." This magic belongs to the sacred feminine that pulls us into life, into appearance after appearance. She is both temptress and teacher.

On the one hand, the seeker must not believe in the illusions of life, or she becomes trapped. And yet life is alive—created by the Absolute to reveal the Absolute—and its illusions can draw us inward towards the Source. "Seize upon the outward, even if it flies crookedly!" wrote Rūmī; "In the end, the outward leads to the inward."[4]

Sufis talk about the world of forms being "secondary causes," which are understood as outer forms of inner realities. For those who believe only in the outer world, these forms are veils of illusion that trap us in an endless maze of attachments and desires. But for those who understand that the outer world is a "secondary cause," these illusions are a path through the maze of appearances—they are signposts towards the Real.

This is why in a living tradition a spiritual teacher may point towards, or illuminate, a particular illusion to help lead the seeker through the maze. As in the story of Zulaikha, whose attraction to Yūsuf eventually freed her from her entrancement with the world of forms, the seeker may need to engage more deeply with the energies of life so life itself becomes the path. "The outer teacher points to the inner teacher and the greatest teacher is life itself." The illusions of life entice, and possibly entangle, but with the right attitude and with the guiding light of Self, the seeker moves through these experiences without being lost in them. The veils of deception gradually become veils of revelation.

But today, there is another set of veils at work—veils that are not designed to reveal, veils that are designed to distort. These veils keep the seeker from recognizing the Real and impede any potential for collective transformation.

VEILS OF DISTORTION

Something has happened in Western culture, and also globally, that is very strange and unique to our time. We have created a series of veils that do not belong to life. These are not veils that lead us to Truth. These are veils of distortion that cover Truth and change form even as we try to see through them. With these veils there is no revelation but more and more distortion. They are veils that deny life its sacred nature and try to draw us ever further into distractions.

These veils exist in an intricate, in-between dreamworld that humanity has created. This imaginary world has infiltrated the collective consciousness and feeds off our light. It has to do with materialism and the distorted belief that meaning comes from material accumulation. It has to do with our greed and the greed of our global corporations. But it would not be correct to blame greed alone. There are extremely dark forces at work that use the power of greed to perpetuate the illusions of our Age.

It is important for seekers to discriminate between these types of veils—the veils that can lead one towards Truth and the veils of distortion that we ourselves have created. The veils that cover most of the world today are not the veils of God. They belong more to our computer-generated culture than to the natural order of creation.

These veils distort almost everything we see and also everything we feel, determining what we want as well as what we think we need. They work with our aspirations and beliefs, and are well designed to make sure one is never going to be free. They have the purpose of keeping the individual imprisoned and spinning continually in a web of constant desires and distorted ideologies without even realizing it.

In contemporary spirituality it is extremely difficult to hold true to one's inner principles, to one's simple longing for Truth, because the moment any energy or grace is given to help a seeker move forward on the path, it easily feeds the collective illusions of life that have taken root in the psyche. The simple, direct perception that belongs to the soul, or Self, has become almost inaccessible. And without direct perception one cannot know where one is, where one is going, or even where one wants to go.

Most seekers do not realize that the inner worlds are saturated with the same darkness that pervades our materialistic society. The veils work with both worlds, weaving the worlds together, strengthening the distortion. Outer-world desires and delusions, patterns of self-interest, and webs of entanglements are reflections of forces and delusions on the inner planes. Today, seekers who follow the ancient traditions of turning inward for the Truth will meet the same veils that cover the outer world.

These veils act very strangely. It is as though they are alive. If one tries to see past them, if one engages an intention to see beyond them, they may start to change and shift into other veils. The illusions then become more refined, more sophisticated. This is because the illusions of the world are interacting with human consciousness. Just as advertising has become more and more sophisticated, utilizing all possible tools to trap us into buying stuff we do not need, so has this web of illusion grown in power and subtlety.

This process of veiling has accelerated in the last years. Like computer games that alter our thinking patterns to increase our addictions, these veils have affected us in ways we do not understand. There is such darkness that often we do not know where we are, and more importantly, we don't even know we don't know. Because of this covering of the light, humanity cannot even begin to take responsibility for what we have done to the Earth, to each other, to what is sacred in life. We do not see how our very way of life contributes to a civilization that constantly undermines everything that is real.

The veils of distortions not only work with our consciousness, they also have a significant impact on the energies of the Earth. Instead of the daily rituals of life bringing light and harmony into creation, as they have in the past, our way of life now contributes to a growing imbalance and degradation. In the same way that our own individual unconscious and the negative forces in our psyche can work with the energies of our bodies to perpetuate or even create illness, so too these veils are working with our way of life to push the world further and further out of balance, making it increasingly sick.

This is an extremely dangerous collusion that is harming not just humanity but the whole of life, inhibiting our collective evolution, undermining the potential transformation of our Age.

THE DARK SIDE OF CREATION

Life is more alive than most of us know. There are energies within the Earth that wake up and go to sleep, that come alive and fade away. Life has its own cycles of creation and destruction. Shamans have always understood how to work with the rivers of life, the deep patterns of life force, just as many indigenous traditions and the ancient Taoists did.

The preeminent Taoist Chuang Tzu told a parable of a wood carver, illustrating a simple way to work with the energies within the material world. In the parable, Khing, the great carver, describes how he created a beautiful bell-stand:

> My own collected thought
> Encountered the hidden potential in the wood;
> From this live encounter came the work
> Which you ascribe to the spirits.

It used to be known how to work with our own attention and the energies of the trees, the plants, the rivers. While modern physics is re-introducing to humanity an understanding of the interdependence of consciousness and matter, that awareness has yet to take hold in the collective. We have forgotten the Earth's inherent powers, and that forgetting—and even more, our resulting treatment of the Earth—has had serious consequences. Our attitudes have not just veiled us from these forces within creation, but have caused us to reject and abuse them. Just as our personal neuroses can repress and damage our own bodies and our life force, so is our present collective pathology damaging life as a whole. The ecocide we witness in today's world—the loss of species, the poisoning of the air and the land and the oceans—is a symptom of this pathology.

Today, many of these forces within creation, these rivers of energy, are constricting and turning against themselves in the way that healthy cells can morph into cancer cells and work to destroy the vital energy of the body. As in the image of the *ouroboros*, the snake eating its own tail, life continues, round and round, but nothing truly new is born—only now this devouring aspect of life's primal realms is becoming more and more empowered and undermining life itself.

The collusion between our collective attitudes about life and the energies of life itself has created a particularly destructive matrix of darkness, a dark magic that veils the light of Truth and distorts what is sacred. Instead of energies from the inner world flowing through creation, nourishing life on this planet, they are co-opted by this net of darkness where they are used to destroy life. Even the light of our consciousness—our most precious gift—is used to create technologies that distort life at a fundamental level rather than nourish the soul. This darkening has left most of us blind or stumbling in the shadows.

But mystics know how to see in the dark.

Mystics are familiar with darkness. The mystical journey often begins with a confrontation with the darkness of one's personal shadow, the rejected and unacknowledged aspects of one's psyche. Then it can take one further, into the darkness of the inner world of the Goddess, the instinctual depths where transformation takes place. This journey is a descent away from the light of the conscious self, into the interior world, where the seed of new growth germinates in the dark.

At this stage of the journey, a seeker might dream of being lost in caves or tunnels beneath the earth, or of descending to the bottom of the ocean where there is no light. From these primal realms, the whole human being is transformed—the consciousness re-woven into the instinctual nature so the light of the soul has new ways of expressing itself through embodied life. In alchemy this is the pearl of great price found at the depths of the ocean.

And the mystic can go even further, into the darkness of the unknown and unknowable aspects of the Divine. This is the *via negativa*, which takes one into "the dark silence where all lovers lose themselves."[5] Beyond the safety of the conscious self are dimensions known only to those who have given themselves to love's undoing, drowned in the vast oceans of non-being.

In such dimensions of darkness, the seeker is lost, her mind bewildered. Here, she is trained to work beyond rationality and reason, beyond the need even to know what she is doing. She has let go into the void, and needs only the light of her own aspiration and willingness to serve.

The capacity to be awake in the depths of our instincts and in the darkness of unknowing is a key to working with the soul of the world today.

But as we stand together at the abyss of collective self-destruction with its unknown consequences,[6] we have to be able to face our fears and our grief at what we have done. Only with an open heart and true awareness can we begin to work again with the energies within creation. Only then can we bring the light of our consciousness into the darkness we have allowed to engulf us.[7]

At this time in history, the darkness of life is actually more present, accessible, and available than the light, which is more veiled, more hidden.[8] The light of our consciousness is also being manipulated to create the ever-changing veils that distort life. As has been said, if we try to engage with these veils, they shift and change, entrapping us anew.[9]

But because these veils, however distorted, are also part of creation, born from a mixture of light and darkness, they also contain the energy of the Goddess—the great primordial realms. And life always contains a seed of Truth.

Life always includes signs that can be read.

All natural things—the life-giving as well as the life-taking, the creative and the destructive both—are doorways to the Absolute.

To redeem life on Earth, to remember the Truth within existence, we need to remember that life is alive, that even as we try to control and dominate the planet, something deep and hidden is still interacting with us. We can call on these hidden feminine forces with their power to create and destroy. The Goddess both veils and unveils; her power can help change the illusions that are siphoning the light and lifeblood of humanity and the resources of the planet. A potent magic that can help reverse this process is right here, held and guarded in her primordial world.

Seekers can work on the inner planes, access levels of light, help humanity from the inner worlds. But if any outer change is to take place, if transformation for the whole of life is possible, it will only happen with the help and power of the Goddess, the guardian of the Earth and all of its inhabitants.

In her hands she holds a fine thread of Truth, slipping it through her fingers like the wool of a skilled spinner. If we approach and honor her, she will give us the end of her magic thread, and like Theseus from the labyrinth we can follow it Home.

How do we do this work? The first step is to recognize the Goddess in her beauty and darkness, the power of her magic, the entrancement of her illusions. The primal power of creation is present in all of her forms, in the beauty of a sunrise as well as the terrible darkness of materialism.

We can take responsibility for how our own lives are a meeting ground for darkness and light, for instinct and consciousness working together. We can acknowledge that what we see all around us—the destruction of the eco-system, obsession with material wealth, the poisoning of our food—is a reflection of complex inner dynamics, of eras of forgetfulness.

We can look straight at our own materialism, questioning why we have projected our longing for meaning and our need to be loved onto the search for more and more *stuff.* We can acknowledge the profundity and absurdity of how our hatred of our own bodies and our fears of being entrapped by nature have undermined any sense of being in harmony with our world.

And we can laugh at how our drive to be free has left us all imprisoned—how what we all truly need is just that which we have rejected.

Spiritual life always has a sense of irony and a sense of humor. The way through the darkness of these times is not to look for light alone, but to recognize the intricate beauty of the darkness, how it points to our own power, how it gives us opportunity for choice, expansion, and for taking responsibility.

Patterns of the objectification of life, of consumption and consumerism, need our pressing attention. The Goddess has bewitched and entangled us, seduced and devoured our light, but we have been more than willing victims.[10] Like Edmund, seduced by the enchanted box of sweets of the White Witch in C.S. Lewis' *The Lion, the Witch and the Wardrobe*, we have allowed this to happen.

There is a way to look within the story of the darkness of this present time, the story of our seduction and betrayal, to find what is real. We need humility to take this step.

And we need the magic of the Goddess—the beauty and power that come from her inner archetypal worlds, from the energies that belong to the names of creation. If we are to "change the story"—from our present self-destructive myth of separation from the Earth into the story of a living, interdependent whole[11]—then it is only from a place of accepting her that we can move forward. We cannot transition into wholeness with patterns of rejection or denial. Or even with the simple forgetfulness of her wisdom and power.

There is a flow of life that belongs to evolution, to the simple miracle of life, and darkness is part of this miracle. Accepting our darkness takes us into the crucible of transformation, and if the process is complete we come always to an experience of wholeness, of oneness. What had seemed like darkness was not just darkness. What had seemed like light was not only light. As in the ancient symbol of *yin* and *yang*, the opposites have always contained one other.

Woven into the veils of distortion are the mystery and beauty of the hidden light of the *lumen naturae*. And so we must honor the material dimension of life—not just the beauty of nature or the abundance of our garden, but also the monstrous materialism that has taken over our world and its magic that has seduced us. We must come to

109

understand this story of the darkening, of our forgetfulness and betrayal of what is sacred within creation.

Only when we bring our longing for Truth into our daily experience and face even the darkest aspects of modern life can the most powerful alchemy happen.

THE VEILS OF DISTORTION AND THE SPARK OF TRUTH

Creation needs intimacy with its Creator. The Creator longs to be united with creation.

If a human being is here to serve the Real, she has the potential to bring together the spark of the Absolute found within the heart with the sacred substance waiting in creation. Our attention and our longing allow the substance in our souls to directly connect to its hidden partner in the density of matter, from our heart to the heart of the world, to the very core of life. In turn, the substance of creation reawakens. Creation comes alive with Truth, and the human being has participated in how the Real expresses Itself through the kaleidoscope of life.

No veils can stop this communion. No distortion can overpower the longing for Truth, which is Truth longing for Itself. When a human being lives in service to the Truth, she can be a catalyst for real transformation.

Creation is waiting in her darkness and her light. The Absolute is waiting in the cells of life, undefiled and completely Itself. It is in a state of great receptivity and expectation. Everything is present and yet not quite in existence. Creation holds all the possibilities of everything that could ever be.

And it waits.

But this receptive aspect needs a spark. Creation needs the spark of the Creator for new life to come, for the Divine to be reborn. And the spark is present in our highest intention, in the love within our heart. It comes from the deepest purpose of our own soul, which is and always has been to love and serve God, to acknowledge that the world belongs to God and that life is essentially sacred.

This great magic of Creator as creation is not other than one's ordinary life, one's deepest humanity, one's breath, one's love and longing. It is here that the book of life is written—in the moment-to-moment intimacy of our breath, our love and longing, as we bring those consciously into our ordinary lives. Too many of us are waiting for something else—extraordinary states, powers beyond our own— or someone else to do the work that is needed.

But we have what is needed always present and available within us. When we live according to the real need and purpose of our soul, its hidden substance can wake up. We do, as Rūmī says, *the one thing needful*. If we fail to live our soul's longing for Truth we will remain caught in the veils of deception and nothing will have meaning; nothing can really happen. The snake eats its tail, grows longer, and continues to eat its tail. Life's distortions grow as its sickness worsens.

But if we follow the thread in the darkness, if we allow the spark of Truth within our heart to guide us, then the real magic of creation will no longer deceive us but will reveal life's secret. Once again the signs of life will speak to us; the mystery and wonder will be present within the ten-thousand things. With open eyes we will be able to see the Real that is all around us:

To meet You I look at face after face, appearance
after appearance. . . . To see Your face I pass by like
the morning wind.

al-Hallāj

It is so simple. And yet, it is the whole of life celebrating
its highest purpose.

8

RETURN TO THE REAL

—◁◁◁∙ℕℕ∙▷▷▷—

He brought me to the banqueting house,
and his banner over me was love.

Song of Songs

Today's world clutters and confuses the psyche and the soul. The veils that cover our daily life prey on our attraction to complexity and our mistrust of the simplicity of life. They distract us from what is most basic, most universal, and most real.

But within this mirage there are a few core human experiences that are still alive, ways to honor the Absolute and return to the Real—the instinct for kindness, for example, or the simple care for another human being. We can still cook a bowl of vegetable soup. We still grieve at the passing of a loved one. We still breathe.

These might not look like the signs pointing to Truth; they are too simple and too ordinary. They do not appear as secret or mysterious. But in our present time this is where the signs of God are to be found—hidden in plain sight.

Today, to align with the Truth on any level requires a willingness to be human, a return to what is essential and most natural. Many of us will need to start again, to go back to the basics. For the last few thousand years we have been convinced that everyday life is not where the Absolute can be known. Our major traditions have focused our attention on the transcendent beyond ordinary life, looked to the heavens beyond Earth, to experiences that take us away from ourselves. They have looked away from the true mysteries of the human heart, its vulnerabilities and openness, its capacity to see the many as the One.

A few traditions have emphasized the ground of ordinary life as a way into these mysteries, and they can be helpful today. The Sufi figure of Khidr exemplifies this aspect of the path. Like Moses, we often pass Khidr by because he appears as someone so ordinary. But in Khidr we encounter the place where the human and divine meet, where the fish comes alive—where the esoteric teachings become a living reality, not something you study in books. When Rūmī met the wandering dervish Shams, the theological professor became love's greatest mystical poet, celebrating the divine that is alive in the heart of everything. When one meets Khidr, the innermost secret becomes life's passion and joy, which the mystic lives in every moment of every day, with every step and every breath.

Zen and Dzogchen Buddhism have also traditionally emphasized this ordinary dimension of life where all levels of reality can come together. The Zen priest Issa devoted his life to his tradition, and yet he never moved away from a willingness to be human. He wrote one of his most famous haikus after the death of his second child:

> This world of dew—
> Is only a world of dew,
> And yet, and yet ...

The vast nothingness, the dimension of divine emptiness, is reflected and known through the impermanence of life—the world of dew—while at the same time the human heart retains its softness, its willingness to feel, its capacity to love and to grieve.

A focus on what is most ordinary and essentially human allows us to breathe, to let go of the distractions of modernity, to see into what is present. Through simplicity we can connect all the dimensions of the Absolute—from the great emptiness of the void to the divine beauty of Earth, the darkness and light of duality and the peace alive in Oneness. If we try to avoid life's ordinariness—if we remain caught in the desire for more and more distractions—we deny the Absolute its opportunity to be known on all levels. We limit the whole of life's moment-by-moment revelation.

The nature of the soul—the individual soul as well as the soul of the world—is a quality of being in which things just *are*. Here peace *is*, love *is*, even power just *is*. We will never notice, let alone really live, these qualities if we follow our desires to escape the ordinary, trapped by the fantasies and dramas that permeate modern life.

A human being who is not scattered by the apparent complexities of life, by its mass distractions, has access to an innate power. When we accept what is most natural, we reclaim the spiritual power that life's illusions so continuously try to drain us of. This power within life is reflected in the haiku of the Soto Zen Buddhist, Ryokan:

> The wind has settled, the blossoms have fallen;
> Birds sing, the mountains grow dark—
> This is the wondrous power of Buddhism.[1]

The profound unification of the nothingness with the ten-thousand things, the bringing together of dimensions of emptiness and ordinary life, is also reflected in the Tibetan tradition of Dzogchen:

The pathless path
Is the path always under our feet
And since that path is always beneath us
If we miss it, how stupid![2]

Even in the 14th century, the counsel to seekers is to not turn from daily life, but to know the Real within it.

But how do we recognize the path under our feet—which might, like Khidr, seem so ordinary that we miss it? Recognizing the path for what it really is has become very difficult in our world with all its distractions and distortions luring our attention away from the simple realities right in front of us, right under our feet. But if we are committed, if we follow our longing, follow the call of the soul, we will be shown what is Real in the ordinary world around us. Our footsteps will guide us. The power of love and the grace that is given will strip away our illusions, leaving us with ourselves just as we are and the world just as it is. It is here that we will find the Real, the pathless path.

T.S. Eliot calls this state,

A condition of complete simplicity
(Costing not less than everything).[3]

It has always cost everything to know and serve the Truth. And perhaps today it is harder than ever to return to the Real. But the keys are given to us and they are the same keys that have unlocked the secrets of the heart and the mysteries of life since the beginning of time—honoring the longing of the soul, surrender, giving ourselves to service, giving ourselves to love. Not to the illusions of love, but to love as it truly is.

LOVE

If human beings are to serve the Real in these times, if we are to work with the world as it is—with the darkness as well as with the light—we need to invoke the deep magic of love. Because as well as being the greatest power in creation, love has a subtle and transformative magic, an ancient magic, that is alive in the connection of lover and Beloved.

There are many, many secrets woven in the threads of love that link us together and link us with God. Love is so much more than an idea or a feeling: it is a living mystery, a mystery that connects all levels of existence and helps us awaken to where we are truly needed.

In the nothingness, love is pure potential. It is present as soon as life comes into being, in that initial explosion of life from which oneness is born; it remains present in the duality of light and dark, beauty and majesty. Flowing out of the emptiness, love is the invisible foundation of creation present throughout all of life, in every feather of every bird, in the ripples of a mountain lake, a tear in the eye of a child. Love is not limited by any level or dimension. It is timeless, weaving the eternal into the present with a hidden thread.

In Sufism, all creation is a story of lover and Beloved. All life longs to know its Creator, longs to return to the Sun from which it came. And Sufism embodies the essential truth that God, the Great Beloved, needs people who can bear His love, an understanding echoed by William Blake:

> And we are put on Earth a little space,
> That we may learn to bear the beams of love.[4]

The Great Beloved needs lovers to share the secrets of divine love, the mysteries of oneness, and the revelations of Truth.

All of humanity carries the memory of this divine love affair, which belongs to the soul. This memory of love does not belong to the personality. It is alive in our longing, in our great need for love, for belonging, for Truth: *Listen to the reed, how it tells a tale, complaining of separation—saying, ever since I was torn from the reed-bed, my lament has caused men and women to moan.*[5]

One might have practiced on a spiritual path for thirty years, or one might be walking through a dappled wood, or one might have just met a friend who will be a friend forever—suddenly love is present, arriving unexpectedly, as a tender feeling, a fragrance in the heart. Love can be found within all of us, and wherever it appears it brings us into the dimension of the soul. With love, we can go behind the veils towards the Truth within the heart, and we can also access the world we are supposed to be living in—the real world, a world of meaning and a world of revelation—a world created out of love.

But we need to remember the real nature of love. In most mystical traditions, to be truly alive means to die. That's why the Sufi says, "Nothing is possible in love without death."

If you cannot die, you cannot fully love. Spiritual life has always been about the death of the ego and the awakening to the perception of the Self or soul, the ocean of love, the shoreless sea where "swimming ends always in drowning."[6]

Even if we have read or been told that the ego "has to go," that you have to "die before you die," we cannot imagine a state in which our "I" is not at the center. Most seekers thinking of the Self imagine a spiritualized ego. We are rarely prepared for the simplicity of what is. The Self may have a cosmic dimension, but it is also the most ordinary and simple essence, a quality of being that is present in everything, identified with nothing—that just *is*. And we cannot begin to comprehend the states of non-being that exist beyond the Self with a consciousness that is centered on its own sense of existence. How can we imagine a state in which we are where we are not? The real nature of the path, unlike everything to do with the ego, is about becoming emptier, having less rather than more. This emptiness within us is a living vehicle for love, a way to witness the Absolute in life.

Externally the lover may remain in the world of multiplicity, but her love for God has merged with God's love for her. In this merging the circle of love is completed. Najm al-Dīn Kubrā describes this state in which the opposites—including the opposites of form and emptiness, inner and outer—have been united:

When the lover is annihilated in love, his love becomes one with the love of the Beloved, and then there is no bird and no wing, and his flight

and love to God are by God's love to him, and not
to Him by him.[7]

Love is within and around all that exists. It is the
thread of the fabric of life, the warp and weft that hold creation together. And yet it is part of love's mystery that it is
continually flowing anew into the world. And it is part of
the mystery of the spiritual path that, in a process that is
very sophisticated and at the same time very simple and
totally elemental, human beings can become a vehicle for
the flow of love into the world.[8] Through our practices,
through the teacher, or through the masters of love working
on the inner planes, our spiritual centers can be activated
to spin at a certain frequency that is aligned with the work
that needs to be done. Love can flow effortlessly through
the heart, and through it into the world.

If we die to the self, we can wake up to this love that is
both all around us and working through us. When we do,
we hear the heartbeat of life. We hear the song of creation
singing the sacred names. It is the seeker's conscious commitment to what is Real, the lover's giving herself to her
Beloved, that allows this surrender of self and opens the
door to the mystery of love.

Surrendered, the mystic is in a unique state of both
total inclusion and total renunciation. This is not a state
of renunciation alone. For in the expanding circle of love,
nothing is left out. The wholeness at the core of our soul is
always present.

In Sufism, this state is described as mystical poverty,
the poverty of the heart whose "inner truth is that the
servant is independent of all except God." Mystical poverty

is the heart's inner attachment to its Beloved, and freedom from all other attachments. It is in this sense that the Sufi regards absolute poverty as absolute richness.

Mystical poverty allows the lover to know the Beloved in the inner and outer worlds. There are no restrictions, for it is the lover's work to look to where the Beloved is, regardless of the form, to live the truth that "God never discloses Himself in a single form to two individuals, nor in a single form twice."[9] Attached to the world of forms, we see the outer shape of creation, a creation that is an empty illusion. But unattached to the world of forms, the eye of the heart sees the secret hidden in all that is, the feminine mystery of creation. In the words of 'Attār,

> If the eye of the heart is open,
> In each atom there will be one hundred secrets.[10]

The heart of the human being opens, and we learn to see with the eye of the heart, listen with the ear of the heart. This is something we have forgotten. It is a great mystery of being human, how our hearts can be opened.

If a seeker is ready, if she has committed to the path, her heart can be turned by the grace of God, by a master of love. It can be breathed on, like an ember that erupts into flames. Then, the seeker *is* the connection between God and creation, a connection that remembers the Divine throughout all levels of existence, that is infused with love and sees and knows the love that is in everything. This love is alive with the knowing of itself; it contains the past and the future, and the knowing of God is present in it. It is a gift of the moment.

121

Divine love is always present, and yet moment by moment it is given anew. It carries life's deepest secret and purpose. The love that is waiting for us, that is being given to us in this moment of our evolution, contains the mystery and the magic of creation. Only lovers can begin to understand these inner workings of love, how the threads of love are woven into life, awakening creation to its own song that is waiting to be sung.

But this love cannot be given if we are focused on ourselves. It is given when the human being looks to the One, when she is open and vulnerable, willing to be used, when she follows her longing to serve—when she is so surrendered in mystical poverty that she is willing to surrender even her own access to love to the needs of the Beloved: "The heart of the lover is held between the two fingers of the Beloved. He turns it as He wills." "Having nothing and wanting nothing," she enters the mystery of the heart, so that she can be used exactly as she is needed.[11]

THE HEART OF THE WORLD

Part of the power of love is the magic of remembrance. Love makes us remember. The lover always remembers her beloved—the one who forgets is no longer a lover. We remember our beloved in the depths of our heart and in the encounters of each day. Everything we touch, hear, see reminds us of the one we love. When we are absorbed in love, everything is our beloved. Through love we also remember our real nature; we remember our source in the Absolute.

And we are not the only ones who remember and love. There is only one love: our love for Truth is the Creator's

love for creation, as well as creation's love for its Creator.
Just as we remember our beloved, everything in creation
remembers its Creator in a constant song of praise. Dhū'l-
Nūn describes his revelation of this reality:

> Whoever recollects God in reality, forgets all else ·
> beside Him, because all the creatures recollect
> Him, as is witnessed by those who experience a
> revelation. I experienced this state from evening
> prayer until one third of the night was over, and
> I heard the voices of the creatures in the praise of
> God, with elevated voices so that I feared for my
> mind. I heard the fishes who said, "Praised be the
> King, the Most Holy, the Lord."

The spiritual body of the Earth has a heart, just as we
do, and when the heart of the world is awake, it sings the
song of remembrance and praise, creation's love song in
which all the names of creation come alive. Love's magic
then flows through the whole of life, going where it needs,
weaving the patterns and harmonies of love. The song of
remembrance sings its way through the darkness, reminding all of creation of its deepest purpose, untangling the
knots we have created in life, bringing remembrance to
places of forgetfulness.

At the moment, the heart of the world is in a deep
sleep, its love song part of its dreaming, part of the world's
dream. But the hearts of lovers are attuned to the song of
love; they feel it in the space between breaths, in the silence
beneath life's sounds. They live their days attuned to this
song; their heart beats its rhythm. They know the deeper
mysteries of love: how love has been given to humanity as a

way Home, how it belongs to a God who is longing to be known and has come up with ten-thousand ways to express Herself. While much of humanity remains unconscious, absorbed in its nightmares of material prosperity, it remains for lovers to stay awake, and through their hearts and daily life to give their love and knowing of the Real back into the cells of life.

From heart to heart, from soul to soul, there is a call and a response. The Earth calls, out of a deep longing in the Earth for its sacred nature to be recognized, for its heart to be seen and known—for the Real to return. When humanity responds, recognizes the Real in life and offers it back to life, the heart of the world can open and all life can begin to sing.

The song of the world will bring healing and joy and laughter. Creation will once again know its own names and its magic will come alive. Then, we will wonder how it could have been otherwise. Then, we will say to our grandchildren, "I remember the days when it wasn't like this. When this magic was missing from the Earth."

Human beings have the opportunity to participate in this awakening, to bring the Real back into life. But there are roadblocks, tremendous forces of darkness blocking the way. The world is covered in enormous self-interest. Collectively we have forgotten the existence of the Real. We have forgotten the vast nothingness and we have forgotten the divinity of all that is. We have forgotten the violent side of God—the divine will that destroys—and we have forgotten the great intimacy of love. We have forgotten the many ways the One expresses Itself, and we have forgotten our role in witnessing that expression.

Who will remember?

Life wants our attention, it wants to speak to us, it wants to tell us its stories. It wants to share with us its mystery and wonder, as well as its terror and darkness. It doesn't need many people. Just as only a few shepherds witnessed the birth of Christ, life needs only a few of us to listen to it, to hear its cry with an open heart.

The Earth listens and it hears; it has language; it has a soul. We are all part of its song of life. If we give thanks, if we allow ourselves to be human, if we attune to the Real, all creation will respond.

There are those alive today who are willing to live the truth that the path is not about us—that the spiritual journey is not personal, but a journey of the Real coming to know itself. These mystics need to acknowledge that they have come with the purpose to serve; they have responded to a call. Spiritually we are all interconnected and our spiritual practice belongs to life itself—nothing is separate. Our remembrance is the Earth's remembrance.

With each breath the mystic can bring the Truth into creation—bring it from the highest planes right down into our manifest world so she can walk in the presence of God, so she can breathe His breath, so she can repeat His name. It is for those whose hearts are open and awake to reclaim the note that has gotten lost, this note of love that knows the Earth as a sacred place, that recognizes that everything is alive with spirit.

The old pond
The frog jumps in
Plop.[12]

That's it.

The soul incarnates into life's essential simplicity. With each breath we bring its mystery into our world, uniting the vastness of the void with the glory of ten-thousand things. We witness a bud breaking open in springtime, a young falcon with its downy feathers before it takes its first flight. We witness the death and the destruction. And we are a part of it all:

> I am the pangs of the jealous,
>   I am the pain of the sick
> I am both cloud and rain:
>   I have rained on the meadows.[13]

The song of mystical love embraces all of creation as it rings from the human heart and from the heart of the world. It is one of the great secrets of humanity, waiting to be lived.

As the prayer says, "At Thy Command only will I carry out the Pilgrimage of Life … For the Love of All Created by Thee, and for Thy glory." It is up to us to offer our lives back to the Real with love—and to wait, and listen, and respond to the friendship that is offered—the friendship with God. The true companionship.

Then we will experience how our ordinary, transient life is part of the great love affair—*is the great love affair.* And we will live each day for love of the Real.

EPILOGUE

A Story of Life's Mystical Secret

—◁⊐⊐⊐⎓⊏⊏⊏▷—

This book tells a story. It is not a "how to" book, not a book of spiritual instructions. It is a story, sometimes an adventure story, always a love story. Like many stories it is part myth, part autobiographical, part simple truth. It is not an attempt to solve any problems, even if it suggests a part that we can play, an offering we can make. It is a story of things that have been forgotten or covered up. If the old libraries had not been burned, the great monasteries in Tibet not destroyed, you would find some fragments of it there.

As with all stories told from the heart, hopefully it will strike a chord, a note of remembrance. It could open a door into a mystery that our present culture has almost forgotten. It is about how the worlds work together, how the love stories of creation are born, and how these threads are woven into our daily life, even if we never know.

In the introduction I described how this is a time of forgetting, when much knowledge has been lost. This story tells of what was before the forgetting, and what has been hidden and never lost. It tells of a secret so simple it is almost unbelievable.

If the prophecies are to be believed, if the signs are correctly read, we stand at a fulcrum, possibly at the beginning of a new era. At any such beginning it is vital to know what to let go and what to keep, what belongs to the age that is dying and what to the one being born. It is like moving house—what do we throw out, and what do we bring with us? There is always the danger that we would try to bring too much, that we would clutter the new space with unnecessary stuff. But there is also the possibility that we would not bring what we need, that something essential would be left behind. This story reminds us of a few things we must not forget—simple, ordinary things, like love and service and an awareness of what is Real.

And like all stories, I hope that it has been enjoyable and not too much of a burden to read. Some of its sentences may not have been so easy to understand, but that is partly because we have forgotten this language of the soul. Behind this story, looking out between the words, is the bond of love that belongs to all that exists. This bond of love is what really matters, is the story I am trying to tell: how within everything is a relationship of love. It is a bond that can never be broken—otherwise the worlds would fall apart. I hope that this story will help you to feel this relationship, this love, a sense of true belonging.

NOTES

OPENING PAGES

1. Quoted by William Chittick, *The Sufi Path of Knowledge*, p. 375.

INTRODUCTION

1. *The Seven Days of the Heart*, trans. Pablo Beneito and Stephen Hirtenstein, p. 43.

CH 1. SERVING THE ABSOLUTE

1. "Burnt Norton," *Four Quartets.*
2. Even with the preparation and guidance of the path, a direct experience of the Divine can be overwhelming, as I experienced in my early twenties. I was awakened on the plane of the Self, and after being immersed in this dimension of bliss and timelessness, it took me many months for my ego-consciousness to reconstellate so that I could have a "normal" life. See *The Face Before I Was Born: A Spiritual Autobiography,* by Llewellyn Vaughan-Lee.
3. Henry Corbin, *Creative Imagination in the Sufism of Ibn 'Arabī*, p. 189.
4. Corporate advertising's manipulative use of images and symbols to foster desires and sell products, without any awareness of their sacred nature, has profoundly distorted the inner world.
5. The Bible, Revelation, 22:1.
6. Quoted by William Chittick, *The Sufi Path of Knowledge*, p. 143.
7. See Vaughan-Lee, "Where the Two Seas Meet," *Fragments of a Love Story*, pp. 161–175.
8. Abū Sa'īd ibn Abī'l-Khayr, quoted by R.A. Nicholson, *Studies in Islamic Sufism*, p. 37 (slightly adapted).
9. "The only thing a person can ever claim for himself is non-existence, which, in religious terms, is to be God's servant. Indeed, Ibn 'Arabī places servanthood at the highest level of human realization." William Chittick, *The Sufi Path of Knowledge*, p. 24.

CH 2. THE HIDDEN FACE OF GOD

1. "Cables to the Ace," *Collected Poems of Thomas Merton,* sec. 84.
2. Ibn 'Arabī describes this by saying that as He reveals Himself through manifestation, so He hides, or veils an essential part of Himself.
3. "Cables to the Ace," *Collected Poems of Thomas Merton,* sec. 84.
4. Human beings occupied a unique position connecting the inner spiritual world of angels and the outer physical world.
5. Gospel of St. John, 10:30.
6. "The Dry Salvages," *Four Quartets.*
7. Thomas Merton, "Cables to the Ace," *Collected Poems of Thomas Merton,* sec. 84.
8. Quoted by Massignon, *The Life and Passion of Al-Hallaj,* vol. 1, p. 285.
9. The Naqshbandi Sufi Master Ahmad Sirhindī has written in detail about "the experience of the existence of non-being" and the degree of annihilation required for the "disclosure of the Essence and the contemplative witnessing of the Essence." Arthur Buehler, *Revealed Grace,* p. 146.
10. *The Life, Personality and Writings of Al-Junayd,* ed. Ali Hassan Abdel-Kader, p. 172.
11. *Say I Am You,* trans. Coleman Barks, p. 27.
12. Radha Mohan Lal is the same Sufi master Irina Tweedie calls Bhai Sahib in her diary, *Daughter of Fire: A Diary of a Spiritual Training with a Sufi Master.*
13. *Tao Te Ching,* trans. Gia-Fu Feng, Jane English, and Toinette Lippe, ch. 11.
14. Paul Reps and Nyogen Senzaki, *Zen Flesh, Zen Bones: A Collection of Zen and Pre-Zen Writings,* p. 53.
15. *Night and Sleep,* trans. Coleman Barks.
16. In Sufism this is called "the station of no station."

CH 3. THE GIFT OF NOTHINGNESS

1. Gospel of St. Matthew, 20:1–16.
2. Ibid., 20:16.
3. For example, outer service from a place of love brings together the temporal and eternal, as in the saying attributed to Mother Teresa, "Small things with great love."

4. Chogyal Namkhai Norbu, *The Crystal and the Way of Light: Sutra, Tantra, and Dzogchen*, p. 112.
5. "He [Man] stands to God as the pupil, which is the instrument of vision, to the eye; and for this reason he is named a Man. By means of him God beheld His creatures and had mercy on them." Quoted by Bhatnagar, *Dimensions of Classical Sufi Thought*, p. 94. In this sense man's coming into existence makes the process of creation complete. Meister Eckhart makes a similar statement, "The eye in which I see God is the same eye in which God sees me. My eye and God's eye are one eye and one seeing, one knowing and one loving." Robert J. Dobie, *Logos and Revelation: Ibn 'Arabi, Meister Eckhart, and Mystical Hermeneutics*, p. 215.
6. Qur'an, *Sūra* 7:172.
7. See Vaughan-Lee, "Chambers of the Heart," *Fragments of a Love Story*, pp. 17–39.
8. Qur'an, *Sūra* 18:61–83.
9. The image of the dead fish becoming alive suggests that this is the place where spiritual teachings become a living reality in the heart and life of the seeker.
10. Miguel Serrano, *The Story of an Indian Pilgrimage*, p. 97.
11. *Julius Caesar*, act 4, scene 3, lines 218–221.
12. The Buddhist environmentalist Joanna Macy calls it "The Great Turning," the shift from an industrial-growth society to a life-sustaining civilization.
13. *The Zen Teaching of Huang Po*, trans. John Blofeld.
14. "A true dervish, as understood by Kharaqānī and his followers, is non-existent; he has experienced *fanā* and lives only through and in God." Annemarie Schimmel, *The Triumphal Sun*, p. 308.
15. Bahā ad-Dīn Naqshband, the Eleven Naqshbandi Principles, goldensufi.org/eleven_principles.html.
16. Quoted by Idries Shah, *The Way of the Sufi*, p. 164.
17. Traditionally the teacher-disciple relationship is needed in order to make the journey beyond the ego. In this one-to-one relationship the teacher is "the ferryman" taking the disciple from one shore to another, from the ego to the Self, and beyond the Self. Sadly today the emphasis on large spiritual gatherings, and the lack of teachers who themselves have made this journey, means that this individual relationship is often unavailable to the seeker.
18. For example, to become a spiritually "awakened" person.

CH 4. ONENESS

1. *Divine Comedy,* XXXIII: 85–87.
2. *Katha Upanishad,* trans. Shree Purohit Swāmi and W.B. Yeats, bk. 2:1.
3. Anne Carolyn Klein and Geshe Tenzin Wangyal Rinpoche, *Unbounded Wholeness: Dzogchen, Bon, and the Logic of the Nonconceptual,* p. 31.
4. "Sky Flowers," quoted by Peter Matthiessen, *Nine-Headed Dragon River,* p. 184.
5. *The Seven Days of the Heart,* p. 44. The attitude of servanthood protects us from the dangers of inflation that can come from the experience of oneness—identifying with the Divine. Ibn 'Arabī also writes in some detail of the "safety in servanthood"; see William Chittick, *The Sufi Path of Knowledge,* pp. 309–331.
6. *Hadīth qudsī,* quoted by Schimmel, *Mystical Dimensions of Islam,* p. 133.
7. William Blake, fragment from "Auguries of Innocence."
8. *The Essential Rumi,* trans. Coleman Barks, p. 36.
9. Most Sufi orders practice the vocal *dhikr (dhikr jalī).* Naqshbandis are known as the silent Sufis because they practice the silent *dhikr (dhikr khafī).*
10. Matsuo Bashō.
11. Adapted from Sarrāj, "there is a *shāhid* in everything, which demonstrates that He is one." Quoted by Hellmut Ritter, *The Ocean of the Soul,* p. 484.
12. *Theragatha,* verse 548.
13. Bahā ad-Dīn Naqshband, from the first of the Eleven Naqshbandi Principles, goldensufi.org/eleven_principles.html.
14. Transcribed by Paul Reps, *Zen Flesh, Zen Bones,* p. 194.
15. Interestingly other Sufi teachings describe the reverse, that the in-breath brings us into the world of creation and the out-breath returns us to the Source:

    The rhythm to which the breathing is subjected is the rhythm of creation and dissolution, of Beauty and Majesty. Breathing in represents creation, that is, the Outward Manifestation of the Divine Qualities, the flowing of the ink from the *Alif* into the *Bā'* and the other letters of the alphabet; breathing out represents the return of the

Qualities to the Essence; the next intake of breath is a new creation, and so on. The final expiring [i.e., the last out-breath of someone at the point of death] symbolizes the realization of the Immutability which underlies the illusory vicissitudes of creation and dissolution, the realization of the truth that 'God was and there was naught else beside Him. He is now even as He was.'
Quoted by Martin Lings, *A Sufi Saint of the Twentieth Century*, p. 159.

16. Qur'an, *Sūra* 2:115.
17. Master Hsu Yun, *Poems on the Oxherding Series*.
18. From *Befriending the Earth: A Theology of Reconciliation Between Humans and the Earth*, Thomas Berry and Thomas Clark.
19. This is similar to the way individuals and spiritual communities have in the past prayed for humanity, or for specific places in the world where prayer is needed.
20. For a more detailed discussion of the "web of light" see Vaughan-Lee, *Working with Oneness*, pp. 101–104.
21. The present "interspiritual movement" is a valuable recognition of the shared values that underlie all real spiritual traditions, how all belong together as a living whole.

CH 5. TWO POLES OF LOVE

1. In Buddhism, unlike other traditions, the duality of emptiness and compassion is known as feminine and masculine, rather than masculine and feminine. Emptiness (or the wisdom of emptiness) is the space of the feminine, whereas compassion—imaged by the Buddha and Bodhisattvas—is the masculine aspect, the living truth skillfully manifesting through creation.
2. Exodus, 3:14, the response God used when Moses asked for His name.
3. Quoted by Bhatnagar, *Dimensions of Classical Sufi Thought*, p. 89.
4. Quoted by Schimmel, *Deciphering the Signs of God*, p. 220.
5. Ibid., p. 226.
6. Genesis, 6:17.
7. Gospel of St. Matthew, 10:34.
8. *Light Upon Light*, trans. Andrew Harvey, p. 79.
9. 1 John, 4:8.

10. *Rumi: Fragments, Ecstasies,* trans. Daniel Liebert, p. 40.
11. Rūmī, "Some Kiss We Want," *Like This,* trans. Coleman Barks, p. 16.
12. From "Sixty Songs of Milarepa," trans. Garma C. C. Chang, Buddha Net's eBook Library: www.buddhanet.net/pdf_file/ 60songs.pdf.
13. *Hadīth qudsī,* quoted by al-Ghazzālī, quoted by Annemarie Schimmel, *Mystical Dimensions of Islam,* p. 139.

CH 6. THE MAGIC OF CREATION

1. "God's Grandeur," *Poems and Prose of Gerard Manley Hopkins.*
2. Mawlānā 'Ali ibn Husain Safī, *Beads of Dew From the Source of Life,* p. 310.
3. Thomas Berry wrote, "The universe is a communion of subjects not a collection of objects."
4. C.G. Jung, *Alchemical Studies (Collected Works,* vol. 13), para. 256.
5. Peter Kingsley, "The Path of the Ancient Sages," *Crossing Religious Frontiers,* ed. Harry Oldmeadow, p. 48.
6. This was specifically enacted in the Roman Empire in 392 AD, when the emperor Theodosius passed legislation prohibiting all pagan worship, and Earth-based spirituality was persecuted.
7. Gerard Manley Hopkins, *Poems and Prose of Gerard Manley Hopkins.*
8. What the Chinese call the "dragon lines," or in England are referred to as "ley lines."
9. See Jules Cashford, "Gaia and the Anima Mundi," *Spiritual Ecology,* ed. Llewellyn Vaughan-Lee, p. 175–182.
10. Quoted by William Chittick, *The Sufi Path of Knowledge,* p. 154.
11. Indigenous people's understanding of the spiritual dimension of creation came more from an instinctual level of consciousness. We cannot return to this purely instinctual oneness with life, but need to reconnect our individual consciousness with life's wholeness, step forward into a new consciousness of oneness.

CH 7. VEILS OF LIGHT, VEILS OF DARKNESS

1. *Hadīth.*
2. *Rumi: Fragments, Ecstasies,* trans. Daniel Liebert, p. 14. Similarly Ibn 'Arabī writes, "Woman is the highest form of earthly beauty, but earthly beauty is nothing unless it is a manifestation and reflection of Divine Qualities."
3. *Jami: Yusuf and Zulaikha,* trans. David Pendlebury, p. 56.
4. *Mathnawī,* III: 526, trans. in Chittick, *The Sufi Path of Love,* p. 22.
5. The Blessed John Ruysbroeck, *Adornment of the Spiritual Marriage.*
6. Any species that willingly destroys its own ecosystem is engaged in pathological self-destruction.
7. Joanna Macy echoes this in her saying, "The most radical thing any of us can do at this time is to be fully present to what is happening in the world." See www.joannamacy.net.
8. Hindu chronology describes the present time as the *Kali Yuga,* the darkest of the four eras of the Earth. *Kali Yuga* is the Dark Age, throughout which human civilization degenerates spiritually.
9. In my own experience, rather than trying to become completely free from the illusions of this present time, it is simpler to accept them to some degree.
10. I sometimes wonder if our addiction to the myth of materialism is partly the revenge of the Great Mother. Our patriarchal culture rejected the sacred feminine, tried to dominate nature, and in revenge she has imprisoned us in her world of matter, spun ever more potent illusions to punish and entrap us. And we are not even aware of what is happening.
11. Many different people are today articulating the need for a "new story" in order to change our world. For example, Joanna Macy speaks of the "Great Turning" as the next step in our collective evolution. But in this important dialogue there appears to be little awareness of the inner power needed to break the spell of materialism, of the fact that conscious awareness and outer action alone are not enough to free us from our entrancement with the mass distractions that surround us. However, Thomas Berry does speak of the need for "a creative entrancement to succeed the destructive entrancement that has taken possession of the Western soul in recent centuries." See "The Ecozoic Era," *Eleventh Annual E. F. Schumacher Lectures,* October 1991.

CH 8. RETURN TO THE REAL

1. *Dewdrops on a Lotus Leaf,* trans. John Stevens.
2. From *Natural Perfection: Longchenpa's Radical Dzogchen,* trans. Keith Dowman, p. 62.
3. "Little Gidding," *Four Quartets.*
4. "The Little Black Boy," *Songs of Innocence.*
5. Rūmī, *Mathnawī,* I: 1–11.
6. Rūmī, *Rumi: Fragments, Ecstasies,* trans. Daniel Liebert, p. 41.
7. Quoted by Sara Sviri, "From Polarity to Oneness in Sufi Psychology," *Jung and the Post Jungians,* p. 208.
8. Every human being can bring love into the world through the simple act of caring for, or loving another. Spiritual practices can dramatically accelerate this process, taking it beyond the personal, becoming an empty space for love to flow into the world.
9. *Hadīth,* quoted by William Chittick, *The Sufi Path of Knowledge,* p. 103.
10. *The Book of Secrets,* trans. Lynn Finnegan, ch. 55, lines 642–3.
11. This is an expression of spiritual poverty, to quote Rūmī: "Last night my teacher taught me the lesson of Poverty: Having nothing and wanting nothing."
12. Matsuo Bashō.
13. Rūmī, "The Soul of the World," *Rumi: Poet and Mystic,* trans. R.A. Nicholson, pp. 182–3.

INDEX

A

'Abd'l-Khāliq Ghijduwānī 52
Abū Sa'īd ibn Abī'l-Khayr 10n
Aboriginal 86
ādāb 32
Adam 87, 91, 94
alchemy, alchemist 83, 89, 94,
    106, 110
anandamaya kosha 55
annihilation (*fanā*) 20, 22, 40,
    46, 132, 133
'Attār 44, 99, 121
Avalokiteshvara 20

B

baqā 20
Bashō, Matsuo 54n, 125n
Bāyezīd Bistāmī 33, 52
Berry, Thomas 60, 136, 137
Bible 30, 87; Book of
    Revelation 5; Exodus 67n;
    Genesis 69n, 87; Gospel of
    St. John 18n; Gospel of
    St. Matthew 30n, 31n, 40,
    69n; 1 John 70–71
Blake, William 50n, 118
bodhichitta 10
Bodhidharma 45
Bodhisattva 10, 66, 135
Brahma 19
Brahmavidya 19

B (breath)

breath v, 8, 9, 51–60, 63, 69, 80,
    111, 114, 123, 125, 126,
    134–135
Buddha 20, 26, 54, 66, 98, 135

C

chambers of the heart 1, 34
Christ 18, 69, 84, 125;
    Jesus 10, 40
Chuang Tzu 104
consciousness of oneness
    47–63, 56, 89, 136

D

Dante 47
dhikr 52, 54, 134
Dhū'l-Nūn 83, 123
Diamond Sutra 98
Divine Names 66, 68
Dogen 48
dreamtime 86
Dzogchen 32, 47, 114, 116

E

Eliot, T.S. 2, 19, 116
Emerald Tablet 83

F

Fakhruddīn 'Irāqī 3
fanā (see annihilation)

G

Garden of Eden 87
great chain of being 17

H

hadīth 67–68, 99n, 121n;
    hadīth qudsī 49n, 77n,
    82
Hallāj, al- 20, 112
Heart Sutra 20
Hopkins, Gerard Manley
    81, 88n
Hsu Yun 59
Huang Po 38

I

Ibn 'Arabī iii, 8, 10, 34, 49, 67,
    92, 99, 131, 132, 134, 137
Ikkyu 72
Indra's Net 90
Issa 114

J

Jāmī 99
John the Divine, St. 5
Judaism 66
Junayd, al- 20
Jung, C.G. 83

K

Katha Upanishad 47
Kharaqānī, al- 39, 133
Khidr 4, 9, 35, 52, 114, 116
Krishna 36

L

Lao Tzu 24, 25
Lewis, C.S. 109
lumen naturae 83, 89, 97, 109

M

Macy, Joanna 133, 137
Mahayana Buddhist 10, 20, 90
manifest world (*'ālam
    al-shahādat*) 4
Merton, Thomas 13, 17, 19n
Milarepa 74–75
Moses 35, 114, 135
Mother Teresa 10, 132
Mundaka Upanishad 33

N

Najm al-Dīn Kubrā 119
names of creation iv, 60, 85–89,
    91, 94–95, 109, 123
Naqshband, Bahā ad-Dīn
    44, 52, 55n, 134
Naqshbandi 41, 44, 52, 132,
    134
Newton 16
nirvana 38
Norbu, Namkhai 32

P

Padmasambhava 9
prana 50
primordial covenant 34

Q

Qur'an 34n, 35n, 57n, 87, 95

R

Radha Mohan Lal (Bhai Sahib)
   23, 36, 132
Rūmī 22, 26, 29, 39, 43, 51,
   70, 71, 71n, 97, 99, 100,
   111, 114, 118n, 119n,
   126n, 138
Ruysbroeck, The Blessed John
   106n
Ryokan 115

S

Safī, Mawlānā 'Ali ibn
   Husain 82n
samadhi iv, 19
samsara v
Sanā'ī 68
Sarrāj 54n, 134
satori 88
Serrano, Miguel 36
servanthood 9–12, 49, 131, 134
shāhid, see also witness 33, 134
Shakespeare 37
Shiva 65
Sirhindī, Ahmad 132
Song of Songs 113
Subhuti 26

T

Taoist 24, 44, 104
Tatanka Yotanka
   (Sitting Bull) 72
Teresa of Avila 69, 99
Tokuson 20
Tweedie, Irina 16, 42, 75, 132

V

via negativa 106
Vivekananda 56

W

witness, witnessing (see also
   shāhid) 33, 34, 41, 54,
   58, 81–82, 105, 119,
   123, 124, 126, 132
world of Mystery ('*ālam
   al-ghayb*) 4
world of visibility ('*ālam
   al-shahādat*) 4

Z

Zen 20, 26, 38, 44, 48, 55, 72,
   88, 99, 114, 115

BIBLIOGRAPHY

Abdel-Kader, Ali Hassan. *The Life, Personality and Writings of Al-Junayd*. London: Luzac & Company, 1976.

Al-Jīlānī. *The Secret of Secrets*. Trans. Tosun Bayrak. Cambridge: Islamic Texts Society, 1992.

Bhatnagar, R.S. *Dimensions of Classical Sufi Thought*. Delhi: Motilal, Banarsidass, 1984.

Buehler, Arthur. *Revealed Grace*. Louisville, KY: Fons Vitae, 2011.

Chittick, William C. *The Sufi Path of Knowledge*. Albany, NY: State University of New York Press, 1989.

—. *The Sufi Path of Love*. Albany, NY: State University of New York Press, 1983.

Corbin, Henry. *Creative Imagination in the Sūfism of Ibn 'Arabī*. Princeton: Princeton University Press, 1969.

Eliot, T.S. *Four Quartets*. London: Faber and Faber, 1944.

Holy Bible. Authorized King James Version. London: 1611.

Hopkins, Gerard Manley. *The Poems and Prose of Gerard Manley Hopkins*. Harmondsworth: Penguin Books, 1953.

Huang Po. *The Zen Teaching of Huang Po*. Trans. John Blofeld. New York: Grove Press, 1994.

Ibn 'Arabī. *The Seven Days of the Heart*. Trans. Pablo Beneito and Stephen Hirtenstein. Oxford: Anqa Publishing, 2011.

—. *Whoso Knoweth Himself*. Oxford: Beshara Publications, 1976.

Jāmī. *Jami: Yusuf and Zulaikha*. Trans. David Pendlebury. London: Octagon Press, 1980.

Jung, C.G. *Collected Works*, vol. 13. London: Routledge & Kegan Paul.

Klein, Anne Carolyn, and Geshe Tenzin Wangyal. *Unbounded Wholeness: Dzogchen, Bon, and the Logic of the Nonconceptual*. Oxford: Oxford University Press, 2006.

Lao Tsu. *Tao Te Ching*. Trans. Gia-Fu Feng, Jane English, and Toinette Lippe. New York: Vintage Books, 1989.

Lings, Martin. *A Sufi Saint of the Twentieth Century*. Cambridge: Islamic Texts Society, 1993.

Massignon, Herbert. *The Passion of al-Hallaj*. Princeton: Princeton University Press, 1982.

Matthiessen, Peter. *Nine-Headed Dragon River*. London: Fontana, 1987.

Merton, Thomas. *Collected Poems of Thomas Merton*. New York: New Directions Publishing, 1977.

Norbu, Chogyal Namkhai. *The Crystal and the Way of Light: Sutra, Tantra, and Dzogchen*. Ithaca, NY: Snow Lion Publications, 2000.

Oldmeadow, Harry, ed. *Crossing Religious Frontiers*. Bloomington, IN: World Wisdom, 2010.

Rabjam, Lonchen. *Natural Perfection: Longchenpa's Radical Dzogchen*. Trans. Keith Dowman. Boston: Wisdom Publications, 2010.

Reps, Paul, and Senzaki Nyogen. *Zen Flesh, Zen Bones: A Collection of Zen and Pre-Zen Writings.* Rutland, VT: Tuttle, 1957.

Ritter, Hellmut. *The Ocean of the Soul: Men, the World and God in the Stories of Farīd al-Dīn 'Attār.* Trans. John O'Kane. Leiden, Netherlands: Brill Academic Pub, 2012.

Rūmī. *Light Upon Light.* Trans. Andrew Harvey. Berkeley: North Atlantic Books, 1996.

—. *Like This.* Trans. Coleman Barks. Athens, GA: Maypop Books, 1990.

—. *Night and Sleep.* Trans. Robert Bly and Coleman Barks. Cambridge, MA: Yellow Moon Press, 1981.

—. *Rumi: Fragments, Ecstasies.* Trans. Daniel Liebert. Santa Fe, NM: Source Books, 1981.

—. *Rumi: Poet and Mystic.* Trans. R.A. Nicholson. London: George Allen and Unwin, 1950.

—. *Say I Am You.* Trans. Coleman Barks. Athens, GA: Maypop Books, 1994.

Ruysbroeck, The Blessed John. *Adornment of the Spiritual Marriage.* London: Dent, 1916.

Ryokan. *Dewdrops on a Lotus Leaf: Zen Poems of Ryokan.* Trans. John Stevens. Boston: Shambhala, 2003.

Safī, Mawlānā 'Ali ibn Husain. *Rashahāt 'Ain al-Hayāt (Beads of Dew From the Source of Life).* Fort Lauderdale, FL: Al-Baz Publications, 2001.

Schimmel, Annemarie. *Deciphering the Signs of God.* Albany, NY: State University of New York Press, 1994.

—. *Mystical Dimensions of Islam.* Chapel Hill: University of North Carolina Press, 1975.

—. *The Triumphal Sun.* Albany, NY: State University of New York Press, 1978.

Serrano, Miguel. *The Story of an Indian Pilgrimage.* New York: Harper Colophon, 1972.

Shah, Idries. *The Way of the Sufi.* Harmondsworth: Penguin Books, 1974.

Tweedie, Irina. *Daughter of Fire: A Diary of a Spiritual Training with a Sufi Master.* Nevada City, CA: Blue Dolphin Publishing, 1986.

Vaughan-Lee, Llewellyn. *Fragments of a Love Story: Reflections on the Life of a Mystic.* Point Reyes, CA: The Golden Sufi Center, 2011.

—. ed. *Spiritual Ecology: The Cry of the Earth.* Point Reyes, CA: The Golden Sufi Center, 2013.

—. *Working with Oneness.* Point Reyes, CA: The Golden Sufi Center, 2002.

Yeats, W.B., trans. (with Shree Purohit Swāmi). *The Ten Principal Upanishads.* London: Faber and Faber, 1937.

ACKNOWLEDGMENTS

For permission to use copyrighted material, the author gratefully wishes to acknowledge: Faber and Faber Ltd., for permission to quote from the extracts taken from "Burnt Norton," "The Dry Salvages," and "Little Gidding" in *Four Quartets,* by T.S. Eliot, Copyright ©Estate of T.S. Eliot; Houghton Mifflin Harcourt Publishing Company, for permission to quote excerpts from *Four Quartets,* by T.S. Eliot. Copyright ©1940 by T.S. Eliot. Copyright © renewed 1968 by Esme Valerie Eliot; New Directions Publishing, for permission to quote from "Cables to the Ace" in *The Collected Poems of Thomas Merton,* copyright ©1968 by The Abbey of Gethsemani. Reprinted by permission of New Directions Publishing Corp.; State University of New York Press, for permission to quote from *The Sufi Path of Knowledge* and *The Sufi Path of Love,* by William Chittick; Al-Baz Publishing, for permission to quote from *Beads of Dew from the Source of Life,* by Mawlana 'Ali ibn Husain Safi, trans. Muhtar Holland; Wisdom Publications, for permission to quote from *Natural Perfection,* © 2010 Keith Dowman. Reprinted by arrangement with Wisdom Publications, Inc., wisdompubs.org; Grove Atlantic, for permission to quote from *The Zen Teaching of Huang Po,* trans. John Blofeld, used by permission of Grove Press, a division of Grove Atlantic, Inc., ©1959; Shambhala Publications, for permission to quote from *Dewdrops on a Lotus Leaf: Zen Poems of Ryokan,* trans. by John Stevens, ©2003, and from *The Crystal and the Way of Light: Sutra, Tantra, and Dzogchen,* by Chogyal Namkhai Norbu, ©2000, and from *Nine-Headed Dragon River,* by Peter Matthiessen, ©1998. Reprinted by arrangement with Shambhala Publications, Inc., Boston, MA, www.shambhala.com; Oxford University Press, Inc., for permission to quote from *Unbounded Wholeness: Dzogchen, Bon, and the Logic of the Nonconceptual,* by Anne Carolyn Klein and Tenzin Wangyal, ©2006; Anqa Publishing, for permission to quote from *The Seven Days of the Heart,* by Ibn 'Arabi, trans. Pablo Beneito and Stephen Hirtenstein, ©2011; Charles E. Tuttle Co., Inc, for permission to quote from *Zen Flesh, Zen Bones,* edited by Paul Reps and Nyogen Senzaki, ©1957; for the excerpt taken from *Rumi: Poet and Mystic,* by R.A. Nicholson ©1995, current copyright holder unknown; Penguin Random House, LLC, for permission to quote from *Tao Te Ching,* by Lao Tsu, translated by Gia-Fu Feng, Jane English, Toinette Lippe, Certain material copyright ©1997, 2011 by Jane English, copyright ©1972 by Gia-fu Feng and Jane English, copyright renewed 2000 by Jane English and Carol Wilson, used by permission of Alfred A. Knopf, an imprint of the Knopf Doubleday Publishing Group, a division of Penguin Random House, LLC.

About the Authors

LLEWELLYN VAUGHAN-LEE, Ph.D., is a Sufi teacher. Born in London in 1953, he has followed the Naqshbandi Sufi path since he was nineteen. In 1991 he became the successor of Irina Tweedie, who brought this particular Indian branch of Sufism to the West and is the author of *Daughter of Fire: A Diary of a Spiritual Training with a Sufi Master.* He then moved to Northern California and founded The Golden Sufi Center (www.goldensufi.org). Author of several books, he has specialized in the area of dreamwork, integrating the ancient Sufi approach to dreams with the insights of Jungian Psychology. Since 2000 his writing and teaching have been on spiritual responsibility in our present time of transition, and an awakening global consciousness of oneness (www.workingwithoneness.org). More recently he has written about the feminine, the *anima mundi* (World Soul), and spiritual ecology (www.spiritualecology.org). He was featured in the TV series *Global Spirit* and interviewed by Oprah Winfrey as a part of her *Super Soul Sunday* series.

HILARY HART, is the author of three books about mysticism with a focus on women and feminine consciousness. She has been on the Sufi path since 1998. Originally from New England, Hilary currently lives in Taos, New Mexico. Her previous books include *Body of Wisdom: Women's Spiritual Power and How it Serves* and *The Unknown She: Eight Faces of an Emerging Consciousness.*

About the Publisher

THE GOLDEN SUFI CENTER publishes books, video, and audio
on Sufism and mysticism. A California religious nonprofit
501 (c) (3) corporation, it is dedicated to making the teachings
of the Naqshbandi Sufi path available to all seekers.
For further information, please contact:

THE GOLDEN SUFI CENTER
P.O. Box 456
Point Reyes Station, CA 94956-0456
tel: 415-663-0100 · fax: 415-663-0103
www.goldensufi.org

Additional Books from **THE GOLDEN SUFI CENTER**
www.goldensufi.org/books.html

DARKENING *of the* LIGHT:
Witnessing the End of an Era

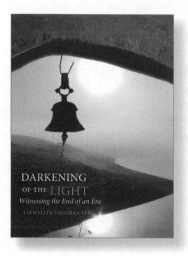

by *Llewellyn Vaughan-Lee*

"I BOW TO THE COURAGE IN THIS BOOK.
Here Llewellyn Vaughan-Lee has
allowed himself to hear the cry of the
Earth. He has been brave enough to face
and to feel the immensity of the loss. He
has dared to share that with us and to
hope we can wake up to save what's left
of our world and our souls."

—JOANNA MACY, coauthor, *Active Hope:
How to Face the Mess We're in
Without Going Crazy*

*The light has sunk into the earth:
The image of Darkening of the Light.*
I CHING – HEXAGRAM 36

Over the last decade or more we have become increasingly
aware of how our materialistic, energy-intensive civilization
has been destroying the fragile balance of the web of life that
has sustained humanity and all living beings for millennia. Yet, while
spiritual teachings tell us that the events in the outer world are a
reflection of changes taking place in the inner worlds, we appear to
have little awareness of how this outer darkening is reflected within.

This book, written between 2004 and the winter of 2012, tells the
story of these inner changes that belong to our spiritual destiny and
the fate of our planet. It is a witness to the darkening of the light
of the sacred, reflected in our continued ecological destruction, and
what this might mean to our shared destiny. With this darkening
comes the danger that we may lose the opportunity for the global
awakening that was possible at the beginning of the new millennium.
This story of our collective destiny, however painful, needs to be
heard if we are to take responsibility for the Earth and reclaim our
sacred role as guardians of the planet.

---

176 PAGES ◈ PAPERBACK: $14.95, EBOOK: $9.99

Spiritual Ecology: THE CRY *of the* EARTH

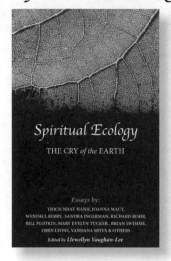

A COLLECTION OF ESSAYS
Edited by Llewellyn Vaughan-Lee

The Zen Master Thich Nhat Hanh
was asked what we need to do
to save our world.
"What we most need to do," he replied,
*"is to hear within us the sound
of the earth crying."*

Our present ecological crisis is the greatest man-made disaster this planet has ever faced—its accelerating climate change, species depletion, pollution and acidification of the oceans. A central but rarely addressed aspect of this crisis is our forgetfulness of the sacred nature of creation, and how this affects our relationship to the environment. There is a pressing need to articulate a spiritual response to this ecological crisis. This is vital and necessary if we are to help bring the world as a living whole back into balance.

Contributors include:
Chief Oren Lyons – Thomas Berry – Thich Nhat Hanh
Chief Tamale Bwoya – John Stanley – David Loy – Mary Evelyn
Tucker – Brian Swimme – Sr. Miriam MacGillis – Wendell Berry
Winona LaDuke – Vandana Shiva – Dr. Susan Murphy Roshi
Satish Kumar – Joanna Macy – Geneen Marie Haugen
Jules Cashford – Bill Plotkin – Sandra Ingerman
Pir Zia Inayat-Khan – Fr. Richard Rohr
Llewellyn Vaughan-Lee

"It's hard to imagine finding a wiser group of humans
than the authors represented here, all of them both thinkers
and do-ers in the greatest battle humans have ever faced.
AN EPIC COLLECTION!"

—BILL MCKIBBEN, founder 350.org

"This gathering of elders from all over the globe … is nothing short
of a modern oracle whose voices translate the wisdom of
the Earth we must care for … Read this book to better
know the irreplaceable ground we all depend on."

—MARK NEPO, author *Seven Thousand Ways to Listen*

---

284 PAGES ❧ HARDCOVER: $24.95, PAPERBACK: $15.95, EBOOK: $10.99

Within the heart of hearts:
A Story of Mystical Love

by Llewellyn Vaughan-Lee

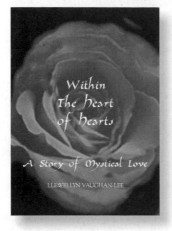

"Sufi Master Llewellyn Vaughan-Lee offers a gentle and uplifting introduction to the mystical ground of being, weaving the voices of legendary Sufi poets such as Rumi, Hafiz, Rabi'a, Ghalib, Abu Sa'id, and Nizami. Reading this book is like sitting in a circle of ancient pilgrims as they share their inner journeys on a mountain at sunrise."

—MARK NEPO, author, *The Endless Practice & The Book of Awakening*

*W*ithin the Heart of Hearts is a journey into the mystical secrets of the heart. Designed to be read like a medieval book of hours, it uses prose, poetry, and images as a series of meditations on the stages of love's mystical journey—from the initial experience of searching and the heart's longing, to the ecstatic union with God, the lover united with the Beloved. This simple but powerful description of the Sufi journey reminds us of this living tradition of divine love.

The popularity of Rumi has shown a thirst in the West for mystical love. This small book is a way to drink deeply of this wine of love, this tradition of lovers of God. Written by a contemporary Sufi, it is based upon a lived experience of the Sufi path and the inner experiences of the heart.

"Llewellyn Vaughan-Lee has a gift. He dives into the deep ocean of classical Sufi teachings, and comes up again and again with pearls of beauty that speak to our hearts today. This is more than merely translating, it is that rare ability to re-present teachings here and now. Recommended for spiritual seekers who are drawn to the path of Divine love."

—PROF. OMID SAFI, Ph.D., Director of Duke University Islamic Studies Center, author, and international speaker

79 PAGES ☙ EBOOK ONLY, ALL FORMATS: **$9.99**
AVAILABLE AS PDF, FIXED-FORMAT EPUB3, OR FIXED-FORMAT KINDLE (KF8)

Additional Books from **THE GOLDEN SUFI CENTER**

www.goldensufi.org/books.html

by LLEWELLYN VAUGHAN-LEE:

PRAYER OF THE HEART
IN CHRISTIAN AND SUFI MYSTICISM

FRAGMENTS OF A LOVE STORY:
Reflections on the Life of a Mystic

THE RETURN OF THE FEMININE
AND THE WORLD SOUL

ALCHEMY OF LIGHT:
Working with the Primal Energies of Life

AWAKENING THE WORLD:
A Global Dimension to Spiritual Practice

SPIRITUAL POWER:
How It Works

MOSHKEL GOSHA:
A Story of Transformation

LIGHT OF ONENESS

WORKING WITH ONENESS

THE SIGNS OF GOD

LOVE IS A FIRE:
The Sufi's Mystical Journey Home

THE CIRCLE OF LOVE

CATCHING THE THREAD:
Sufism, Dreamwork, and Jungian Psychology

THE FACE BEFORE I WAS BORN:
A Spiritual Autobiography

THE PARADOXES OF LOVE

SUFISM:
The Transformation of the Heart

IN THE COMPANY OF FRIENDS:
Dreamwork within a Sufi Group

THE BOND WITH THE BELOVED:
The Mystical Relationship of the Lover and the Beloved

⌒

EDITED *by* LLEWELLYN VAUGHAN-LEE
with biographical information by SARA SVIRI

TRAVELLING THE PATH OF LOVE:
Sayings of Sufi Masters

⌒

*For additional authors and publications,
please visit ww.goldensufi.org*

For Love of the Real

A Story of Life's Mystical Secret